THE
ULTIMATE
FAMILY
BUSINESS
SURVIVAL
GUIDE

THE
ULTIMATE
FAMILY
BUSINESS
SURVIVAL
GUIDE

PRIYANKA GUPTA ZIELINSKI

PAN

First published 2021 by Pan
an imprint of Pan Macmillan Publishing India Private Limited
707, Kailash Building
26 K. G. Marg, New Delhi 110 001
www.panmacmillan.co.in

Pan Macmillan, The Smithson, 6 Briset St, Farringdon, London EC1M 5NR
Associated companies throughout the world
www.panmacmillan.com

ISBN 978-93-90742-00-4

Typeset in Minion Pro by R. Ajith Kumar, New Delhi
Printed and bound in India by
Replika Press Pvt. Ltd.

To my children Henry, Radhika, and Savi

CONTENTS

FOREWORD

AS BUSINESSES ACROSS THE WORLD DEAL WITH THE fallouts of a global pandemic, *The Ultimate Family Business Survival Guide* arrives as an insightful and practical guide for family businesses both small and large. The book offers a range of tips for such businesses to survive, flourish, and even find an opportunity in a crisis post one of the world's toughest global economic crises. Priyanka Gupta-Zielinski's book is also a timely reminder that India's post-pandemic economic recovery will, in a large way, depend on the survival and success of family-run enterprises, which form the majority of businesses in the country.

As a business student, an experienced entrepreneur and especially as someone who is part of a family business, I am confident that this book will be highly beneficial to you for the insights it provides, as Priyanka offers a unique family business model that can aid all sorts of business enterprises in good times and bad. It is also interesting to see how keenly observant Priyanka has been of her father's entrepreneurial journey and how much wisdom she has been able to share from those experiences. The references to her father's journey and the lessons she has derived from it offer perfect examples of how much more can be achieved when different generations come together at work and how traditional wisdom complements new-generational curiosity.

Generational knowledge that comes from working and living within a family business surely sets the foundation for success for future generations. The older generation, while mentoring with a heavy hand, guides from a place of experience and wisdom which the next generation should recognize. I know that many of my ways of doing business are derived from both subtle and non-subtle cues provided by my father. He taught me that to build something that will leave a legacy for generations to come, one must have a relentless spirit to chase success and build a business out of passion. He has shown me that if you care about your business, your passion will pass on the lessons of success to the next generation automatically, and I hope that the way I have run my business for the last few decades will provide the right examples for the next generation.

The family business does also come with its usual inter-generational conflicts that are not often discussed or brought to the forefront of any conversation. Priyanka, fortunately, has done just that in this book – highlighting the importance of each member of a family business having a defined role and telling us why the founding generation should build an organizational framework that creates roles for the new generations entering the workspace.

The book is an easy and enlightening read, and will also help the reader understand, appreciate and differentiate between a family business and a non-family business. I look forward to seeing this book well appreciated and helping us acknowledge the important role family businesses play in society and towards building a strong economy.

Sajjan Jindal
Chairman and Managing Director, JSW Steel Ltd

1

WHY MY FAMILY BUSINESS MATTERS

When I Needed a Flashlight in Daylight

HE SAID WITHOUT PREAMBLE, 'SHEENU BETA, IT'S TIME TO come home.'

It had been six years since I left home to study in the US in 2002. All those years, my father would call me every day, sometimes with a joke, but always with an update on our family business MPIL Steel Structures Ltd, a steel building manufacturing company headquartered in Mumbai. In the fall of 2007, however, he had begun to sound particularly tired during our conversations. When he asked me to return and join him in running the business, it was not a plea, but a long-drawn-out sigh, as if his efforts had failed but he wanted to try one last time.

I was due to graduate from my master's programme at New York University in May 2008, but I didn't hesitate. I instantly said yes to him, noticing the sense of urgency in his voice. With support from the NYU faculty, I moved my classes and exams into an accelerated schedule. I compressed a semester's worth of reading lists into days and changed submission dates to suit my flight schedules. I made time between November and May to shuttle between New York and Mumbai, until I moved back permanently in June. This back and forth between my international finance classes in New York and my 600-square-foot office in Mumbai marked the beginning of a personal exploration of my position at the nexus of my family life and our business amidst a largely conservative Indian setting.

This was a time of great anxiety. I was tormented by several questions. What would I do in Mumbai? What would I do in my father's office? Would my parents even let me go to work? Would I be allowed any independence? Would I be able to take decisions on my own? Would I be allowed to return to the US if I felt dissatisfied in Mumbai? These questions kept haunting me and I was a nervous wreck by the end of it.

For the first few months back in Mumbai, I simply observed everything around me – mostly listening to my father recount his business stories and watching him in action when the opportunity presented itself. My father, Ashwani Gupta, lightens a tense situation with his Haryanvi jokes and idioms, as he confidently applies his do-or-die spirit to every venture he undertakes. On rare occasions, he allowed me to attend meetings outside the office with him, instilling both excitement and pride within me. It was as though I was walking about with a figurative flashlight, seeing and understanding better, capturing, and processing, asking questions as I tried to make sense of it all. At that time in India, there was an acute emphasis on 'building' in every sense of the word: building infrastructure, enterprise, technology, even skills. Today, I realize that those early months, after I had just moved back to India, was the coming-of-age for our business. It was a time when the personal and the professional were fully integrated, and as my father and I dove deeper into the Indian manufacturing ecosystem, we found ourselves being pushed around by the big fish in the industry. We lost some self-esteem, but we also developed a thicker skin, and my father and I re-emerged as an unstoppable duo. We discovered our strengths through our interactions in the office, the factory, during long car rides and with other stakeholders within the steel industry. But we did continue to struggle with channelling our newly acquired knowledge and experiences into the creation of useful, implementable tools to grow our business.

In the late nineties, my father had identified a business opportunity within logistics to shift raw materials inside large integrated steel plants. This was the beginning of our legacy company Pratham Transport Logistics. We used earth-moving machinery such as excavators, wheel loaders, dumper trucks, trailers, and cranes to transport iron ore, limestone, manganese, steel pellets, steel coils, and various minerals associated with raw steel manufacturing. But soon I realized that our business was a string of disconnected work contracts tied together by my father's innate inclination for *jugaad*, a popular Hindi word that 'roughly translates as an innovative fix; an improvised solution born from ingenuity and cleverness'.[1] With his sharp instincts and business acumen, he had transformed his logistics business into a successful profit-making venture, but one still rough around the edges. Despite that, my father's success had gradually lifted our family into the upper middle class within a few years.

Leveraging the success of his logistics business, my father set out to delve into another opportunity in the steel value-addition space. He conceptualized a manufacturing business that had the potential to scale up for decades in the future. He founded MPIL Steel Structures Ltd, a manufacturing house for engineered metal structures, such as factories, warehouses, airports, high-rise and low-rise buildings, power plants, bridges, and metro rails, in 2005. When my father asked me to return to Mumbai, in 2007, the company was a three-machine manufacturing set-up, producing seventy-five tonnes of steel structures every month. By 2017, we had grown to ship 3,000 tonnes of finished, complex steel structures every fortnight.

This book is the story of a family and its business coming of age together, a story of how everything we had once thought impossible for our family business became possible.

2008: The Year I Found My Multipurpose Hat

The year 2008 was a rather (in)famous year for most of us around the world. For me, it was also to be the year of relocation and rediscovery: I had moved to India and joined the family business. Our steel structure business manufactured Lego-style steel components, shipped them to the project construction site, where they would be bolted together as per design. It was the way most construction happened in developed countries and was relatively new to India at the time. For those familiar with the industry, it is called pre-engineered metal construction, because all aspects are pre-planned such that there is an efficient flow in on-site work.

In mid-2008, India began to feel the first jolts of the global economic recession. By October, the country's benchmark indices had fallen 50 percent from January-levels that year, while the Indian rupee had slumped to a six-year low. This financial strain caused the infrastructure sector to decelerate. India has long suffered from an infrastructure gap, and its transport and energy networks have been unable to meet its rapid rate of urbanization. At the time, India's infrastructure ranked 72nd out of 133 countries in the World Economic Forum's *Global Competitiveness*

Report for 2008-2009. The steel industry's attempts to address the infrastructural gap were rendered insufficient in the face of the economic crisis. An acute shortage of cash for capital expansion projects hit us. Furthermore, since large importers such as Europe and the US could not commission their own projects as planned, the recession also caused a slowdown in exports of value-added steel products from India. Then in November 2008, Mumbai – India's commercial capital – was hit by a devastating terror attack. Besides the tragic loss of life, the attack marred India's image as an attractive investor destination.

The recession drove down the prices of steel drastically; with demand slowdown, infrastructure projects that consumed the most steel structures began to stall. Payments from creditors were delayed and the cash-flow crunch began to close in, making daily operations challenging for us. Apart from the recession's impacts on our business, our small team of employees had neither specific job descriptions nor designations, and were mostly jacks of all trades and, unfortunately, masters of none. As the year progressed and its catastrophic effects continued to manifest themselves in various ways, I was reminded of a Hindi proverb – *kangali mein aata geela* – which means that everything takes a bad turn during adversity – a desi version of Murphy's Law. But there was also a glimmer of hope. Since we were a dwindling business, there was no other way we could go but up.

We underwent a period of difficult introspection, something that my father had not previously conducted, to arrive at a significant breakthrough that shook the foundations on which our business was being conducted. We had to take a long hard look at the status quo to figure out what would make us more cost-competitive and how we could manufacture with better accuracy and quality. Our set-up, then, was small with limited machines and technical expertise. A key component of our business, design, and engineering, which determines how much load a structure can bear with the most optimal use of steel, was outsourced to an external firm.

We needed to evolve, retain our strengths, and quickly catch up with the modern manufacturing techniques of the steel industry. We spoke to several experts and veterans in the industry to do our research, since hiring a consultant for help was not an option, given that cost-cutting was our prime focus at the time. The industry had progressed, but we still operated according to old-school rules. My father had correctly sensed that the business would be unsustainable if we did not adapt to the changes. Trusting his instincts, he took the tough decision for a complete overhaul. In hindsight, I now know that his phone call asking me to return was a do-or-die moment for our family and our business.

We decided to create our in-house design team so that we had better control over optimizing the use of steel in a building. This also gave us an edge when it came to bagging orders since many smaller contractors who needed our steel didn't have design capabilities of their own. Similarly, we switched to smaller-capacity machines and focused on acquiring a wider range of machines. Prior to this, we had fewer machines, which were rather heavy-duty and expensive. Earlier, the name of the company was Multicolor Projects, but this name did not immediately indicate what our actual product was. So we tweaked our company's name and re-branded it as MPIL Steel Structures Ltd to present a new version of ourselves to our clients.

There were many firsts in that year of 2008: our first functional company website, our first recruitment drive and our first articulation of a hazy strategy to achieve a nebulous target. To keep the business going, we needed to keep the factory running with a regular stream of orders. This was easy enough to understand, but the question was how to do so in the face of challenging economic times? On the factory floor, I wore a hard hat (helmet) for safety, while continuing to rely on my figurative multipurpose hat as I switched from one role to another, at the factory, at the office and at home – sometimes watcher and at times doer.

My own induction into the business began with staff recruitment, weekly trips to our factory in Tarapur (110 kilometres north of Mumbai) and assuming control of the operational finances of our company. Just the process of conducting interviews helped me learn a lot as candidates shared insights into the market scenario, upcoming demand and hot areas to get orders from. Using our existing relationships with the clients of my father's logistics business Pratham Transport Logistics, we began to offer our steel structure services to plants where we were already a logistics contractor. This helped us use available resources, lean more on our existing employees, and coordinate the progress of the construction closely.

Every little task and every new endeavour had a tremendous impact on our growth. I realized just how many different hats I had to wear in the span of one day, from manager to subordinate, or from artist to writer. After just a couple of months of completing our new website, we began to receive leads via emails. With an in-house design team, we were better positioned to respond to those leads with detailed technical proposals. Each new hire added significantly to our productivity. It was rewarding to experience such hyper-productivity with positive and visible results.

During the week, my father and I would be swamped with operational work. Every Sunday, we would drive to a quiet office to work on business development, to brainstorm, research, and write down plans. During those months, I learned about each aspect of our business in great detail. Even today, people in the steel industry are often surprised by my technical knowledge of our products. I had learned from my father that the savings were in those tiny technical details. Why use 0.65 mm thick steel when 0.49 mm thick steel can be perfectly suited for the job (that's more than 30 percent savings in the material used right there). I also learned the value of persistence, in showing up every day every week to work, and in being a tad patient. In December 2008, we had bagged our first sizeable order that would keep our factory busy for the next two years. Since then, we have never looked back.

Using a Swiss Army Knife to Run a Steel Factory

My father has been my idol all my life. I have sought out opportunities to spend time with him, and the fact that he now trusted me with the business he had worked hard to build said volumes about his belief in me. The thrill of living independently in a different country is different from the exhilaration that comes from being perceived as dependable at home. Here, my father was entrusting me with the MPIL platform – a proud moment for me. But then, I was also afraid I would let him down. In the beginning, I sought his approval for all my decisions. Our business had entered phase 2.0 as a father-and-daughter partnership. I was ready with my Swiss Army knife, a set of tools to help me adapt and course-correct as we geared up for the next stage. We needed to strategically invest in our collective ability to own and manage a business. Now that we were back on our feet, we needed to develop a new vision as to how the business could grow.

Two years after my return, in 2010, my brother, an Ivy-League-educated lawyer, joined the business and brought with him a set of complementary skills that made the three of us a formidable team. My father is a natural firefighter, the eternal problem-fixer who operates on autopilot. My brother is detail-oriented, prescient, and methodical, while I am determined, curious, and willing to experiment. We may fight and quibble all day long like any other family, but we let the emotions play themselves out and then cut through it all to achieve our goals.

In our minds, we had already imagined what our company would look like in the next five years: a full-fledged steel fabrication house, one that could act as a one-stop shop for anyone looking to build a factory or warehouse. Simultaneously, we had begun to accept unique and challenging projects across the power, cement, aviation, and railway industries. For each target, we would begin by preparing several versions of plans and actions, a fail-safe approach for success against all odds. We began to work backwards from our vision of the future so that we could put in place what we needed to get there. It felt as if we were learning to drive and fixing our car at the same time, while we raced against others on the track!

For each new project order we bagged, we relied less and less on outsourcing and began to add machinery and expertise in-house. We were adapting constantly as a company as each new order helped create products of the highest quality for our clients. And personally, I was learning and growing faster than ever, adding new tools to my Swiss Army knife while at work in our factory.

Our clients were supportive and generously shared their technical expertise. From the JSW Steel Group, we received pilot orders that allowed us to provide proof of concept and showcase our ability to deliver. From Eversendai Corp, a leading international steel fabrication firm, we learned ways to improve the quality of the steel beams we manufactured. Our health and safety standards improved considerably under the guidance of Zuari Italcementi (an Indo-Italian joint venture with cement manufacturing plants in Karnataka and Andhra Pradesh at the time). Their detailed checklists on how to safeguard workers during extreme weather conditions inspired us to up our game at all our construction sites.

As a bespoke operation tailored to the demands of each of our clients, we were able to cater to their requirements specifically. For instance, when a new sixty-three-floor residential building in South Mumbai required a certain kind of steel floor deck, we built an entirely new cast for the project, which was later added to our existing machine.

By adding new elements to suit different kinds of steel structures, we were able to ensure that our products complied fully with our clients' needs. We were building an actual and metaphoric armour of machines and skills with the support of the steel community.

Our nimbleness and ability to respond to our clients' demands helped us foster relationships with India's largest business houses and industrial groups, many of whom continue to work with us today. About 85 percent of our orders come from the same network of clients even today, a figure we are incredibly proud of. This is also one of our strengths as a family business.

Between 2008 and 2016, MPIL was my professional university, my very own business school. Here I grew into a business leader and achieved the compound annual growth rate of 550 percent in revenue. I helped build a brand-new LEED Gold-certified manufacturing facility and led our business into the renewable energy sector. I also set up MPIL & the Arts to support public art engagement projects using steel. I made close friends at work and won the respect of my clients and suppliers in the steel industry. Through all this, I also learned how much failure hurts, how difficult it is to pick yourself up again and how high the stakes are when others' livelihoods depend on the decisions you make. I have come to realize how forgiving a family business setting can be; the support I received from my parents, my brother, and my colleagues at MPIL helped me grow as an entrepreneur.

Family Businesses Don the Superhero Cape

Family-managed businesses hold the key to the future of India. They are the 'backbone' of our economy, ranging from the corner *kirana* stores to the multi-billion-dollar enterprises – accounting for 85 percent of all Indian companies – which contribute to 79 percent of our GDP.[5] The Wadia Group, established in 1736, had received its first contract from the East India Company to build ships and docks. The Birla Group (1857), the Tata Group (1868), the Murugappa Group behind the famous Dabur products (1884), are some examples of the legacy of family businesses in India that have stood the test of time and contributed to centuries of Indian growth.[6] By preserving their legacy, they have played an essential role in passing down values and learnings from generation to generation.

Family businesses have historically remained bullish about their growth plans and have often benefited from a motivated founder supported by his family unit and aligned with a core value system. As per a 2013 PricewaterhouseCoopers survey, more than 50 percent of family business owners in India plan to pass their business onto the next generation with as few as 4 percent willing to sell it.[7] These numbers give us just a glimpse of how important these businesses are for the economy. Their immeasurable value in community and family-building compounds their national significance.

In my interactions with my friends and other second-generation family business owners, I started to see that our stories overlapped. A pattern began to emerge, and I got increasingly interested in documenting how family businesses operated in India. In 2010, I began conducting structured interviews to gather quantitative and qualitative data, drawing from the collective experience of family businesses in India. Often unknowingly, family businesses display a natural ability to break down complicated situations into simpler steps. Since they exist in emotional and logical flux, family businesses thrive by mastering the skills to take decisions in a continuously changing environment. Built on research, data, and interviews, my findings reveal the strength that lies in the in-built mantras of management within family businesses. Family businesses play a tremendous role in safeguarding cultural legacy, in local community-building, and in keeping the family unit together. They are also the vehicles of change that can bring about the most impactful economic transformation in our country, given how large their market share is, in terms of revenue contribution, and in creating employment in India.

As I reflected on these experiences, I realized that family business owners, such as my father, are real-life superheroes. They act with courage, in the face of so much uncertainty and change, and continue to offer the youth of India an ideal platform for personal and professional growth, complete with a host of opportunities. For instance, family businesses can serve as incubators for social innovation and progress, allowing the youth to contribute to their communities and manoeuvre societal restrictions. Moreover, a family business can be a safe space for them to express their identities, letting them fall back on the stability of family ties in the face of insecurities that often come with a new job or at the start of a professional career. From these businesses, we learn how parent-child partnerships can operate successfully, about the value of cultural legacy, and how to align individual identities with niche business activities.

Family businesses can become fashionable and unleash their potential if given a chance. They can be both a serious career option for young Indians as well as a critical economy booster at local, regional, and national levels. The lack of formal systems or processes or the chaotic decision-making does not have to be a deterrent. Rather, the way such businesses run on trust, leverage interpersonal relationships, and survive economic downturns, is noteworthy.

Western management principles often critique such unconventional approaches as being 'unprofessional' or lacking in tried-and-true systems and processes. Such a negative perception is further strengthened by the increasing number of Indian youths who go abroad to complete their higher education and return with apprehensions about home-grown business practices and ideals. They tend to deconstruct family businesses through the lens of Western management structures, tossing all local structures aside. As Ruchir Sharma, Head of the Emerging Markets Equity at Morgan Stanley, says, '[O]thers claim India can't sustain tough reform because its people are not disciplined and predictable like the apparently dull East Europeans. Indians are more chaotic, colourful, and moody. But economists used cultural explanations to write off Mao's China in the 1960s as a Confucian society too wedded to traditional ways to modernize fast and look how that turned out.'[8] This is exactly what's happening with family businesses in India; they are less understood and far less credited for their actual contribution to our country.

In fact, family businesses are often more profitable and create more employment than their non-family counterparts. A study conducted by S&P, involving 500 companies, titled 'Family Firm Performance: Further Evidence' found that the average profit margin for family-run firms was 10 percent, 2 percent higher than non-family firms. The study also examined employment trends during the 2001 recession and found that while non-family firms typically downsized during this period, family firms expanded employment by an average of 3.4 percent.[9] Family-run businesses have the potential to empower their employees. For them to do so, we need to replenish their energy and enable their longevity by reminding the next generation to use their own superhero cape.

The Ultimate Family Business Survival Guide is an account of my own personal and professional journey and the dilemmas I faced at home and work. Though I use MPIL as my primary example, my experience will resonate with many others who lead or work for family-managed SMEs (small to medium-sized enterprises). I discuss in detail learnings from my father, his worldview and principles, his do-or-die spirit, and his oft-repeated Haryanvi jokes. In the span of two decades, my father has built two successful businesses (in logistics and manufacturing), with a presence in eleven Indian states and four countries. Some of India's finest infrastructure projects stand on steel structures built at our factories from the monorails and airports in Mumbai to the metro in Chennai to the National Thermal Power Plant in Gadarwara, Madhya Pradesh.

Over the years, with his direct involvement, my father has earned the trust of his clients, many of whom continue to do business with us today. And because of how much he cares for his own people, the average term of an employee at our organization is seven years, the range being from the new recruits to those who have been with us for twenty-six years. He has a team of 1250 workers and knows many of them by name. My father's journey from zero-to-hero is rife with failure and learning, rise and fall, humility and courage. The growth in revenue has always been amplified by the improvement in the lives of his team members and their socio-economic upliftment. As unique as this story is to him, it is also a representation of many first-generation business owners in India, who like my father, have started from scratch and built noteworthy organizations. And that is why our story matters.

This book is primarily for families engaged in business in India. It is for the parent who hopes their children will add their entrepreneurial contributions to existing firms, and for the children who are enthusiastic about creating value, adding entirely new products or services, fine-tuning time-tested processes, and venturing into new markets. It will also be useful for the younger generation that is unsure about whether they want to join their family business at all, and for the parent struggling to figure out how to be a role model to their children in the complicated world of business. It is for the son-in-law or the daughter-in-law trying to figure out their place within their new family and its business. For older generations, this book will serve as a guide for succession planning and increasing managerial bandwidth. For younger generations, it will provide the tools to launch themselves and their aspirations within the realm of their family's business. Cutting through modern-day management jargon, it reveals the inherent entrepreneurial knowledge and power of family businesses.

Lastly, this book is for my own family: my parents, my brother, my husband, and our three kids. I have written it to pass along the learnings of my father and our Haryanvi heritage. It is precisely this relationship of the family with businesses, the confluence of successes and failures and the power of resilience I explore in this book. I write it with my personal inclination toward jugaad, and to help others appreciate and draw from the inner workings of SMEs and their potential for growth.

Inside the Ultimate Survival Guide – Your Parachute to Take the Leap

The book begins with an exploration of the stereotypes surrounding Indian family businesses and shows that these stereotypes – far from holding the businesses back – give them an advantage in the market. Family businesses are susceptible to several types of ups and downs, but they do not have to spell disaster. They are susceptible to additional risk as they must balance the interests of the family and the business, which do not always necessarily align. In the pages that follow, I provide solutions to such risks as well as ways in which they can be negotiated, particularly when our internal fears become a hindrance to progress. Next, I lay out the specific role of family businesses in the post-pandemic world by drawing on previously discussed concepts and solutions. I also highlight the need for policy support from the central government level which could help resolve internal conflicts and execute succession plans smoothly within such businesses.

Wisdom from my father's Haryanvi upbringing and his favourite idioms can be found throughout the book. I hope these serve as a source of empowerment for everyone, just like they have for me, given that they make you reconsider popular stereotypes, bring levity to difficult situations and also act as simple hacks to survive and thrive in the world of business. Just like family businesses, Haryana – a relatively small state – has been undervalued and stereotyped, despite the outsized impact it has had on Indian business and growth. Haryana's culture of entrepreneurship becomes all the more visible if one takes a look at India's top business families – to name a few, OP Jindal Group, Zee TV Group and Welspun Group. What they all have in common is their fearless dedication to get things done.

This book also offers a unique toolkit, the descriptions of which are peppered with examples, adages, and Haryanvi idioms. These creative and flexible tools can help develop a sustainable framework to empower multiple generations in a family business. They are briefly described below.

 Multipurpose Hat: To undertake multiple roles

 Flashlight: For clear vision and deeper understanding

 Superhero Cape: For the guts to push past our fears

 Swiss Army Knife: For course correction and adaptability

 Emergency Parachute: For the do-or-die spirit

Come along with me to explore these tools in detail, and I assure you they will be as helpful to you as they have been to me.

2

WHY ALL FAMILY BUSINESSES MATTER IN INDIA

MORNINGS IN OUR HOUSEHOLD WOULD OFTEN BEGIN with my father telling me, '*Beta, ek letter type kariyo* (Please type out a letter).' I would sit at the computer, and my father would pull up a chair next to me. We would then begin working through a complex business proposal and bring it down to a page. The letter would always have to be one page, never longer. My father believes an idea must be presented in a simple and precise manner, and that no person who is important enough to decide on a contract has the time to read more than a page.

My brother and I, with our strong command of English, have been assisting our father with business communications since we were teenagers – from emails to letters to presentations. These documents needed to be emphatic and precise. But in effect, all we did was to make small corrections as our father dictated the contents of the documents to us, mostly in English. (Although my father had studied in a Hindi-medium school, he had taught himself English over time.) We would then format the documents and make them look professional, but had little input for the contents. Rather, these drafting sessions were a time for us to come together as a family to deliberate and determine how to advance our business and ourselves through the power of language. Whenever my father received compliments for his presentation, he made sure to pass on the praise to us.

The dynamics of our family were relatively uncomplicated. Our father, the leader of our household, charted out our lives. Our mother, his foot soldier, was relentless in her pursuit to ensure that his plans succeeded. The two children were always up for the ride. We were regularly confronted with the realities of our lower-middle-class status, and forever vulnerable to the fear of being replaced in the society in which we were trying to establish ourselves. Yes, our family and the business took a top-down approach, sometimes rife with emotion-driven decisions, but it has worked for us. Most of my father's professional decisions were talked over at home where we sifted emotions, intentions, actions, and words together. Each decision was an energetic attempt to launch our family upwards on the social and economic ladder.

The top-down process where the patriarch takes all final decisions, however, was a veneer, as it is with all family businesses, which at first glance may seem somewhat outdated to modern management practitioners. This approach is often facilitated by significant bottom-up inputs from various family members. A strong top-down leadership, complemented by bottom-up participation and feedback, in such businesses gives business owners the ability to accommodate cultural, familial, and intergenerational intelligence that enables them to succeed. By incorporating the voices of other family members, such businesses allow for high functionality. In this chapter, I will draw out these nuanced strengths of Indian family businesses to help illustrate this process in practice.

In the insightful book, *The India Way*, the authors highlight that the Indian way of conducting business is rooted in 'purpose, pragmatism, and people'.[1] The presence of a strong business leader, who is able to harvest fresh ideas, implement quality execution, and deploy jugaad organization-wide to get things done, has worked for Indian businesses. An overwhelming number of businesses, according to the book, were indeed family businesses. Therefore, as Nikhil Prasad Ojha, partner at Bain & Company, explains, 'It's important to imbibe the learnings of the founders' mentality to thrive.'[2] According to Ojha, there is a need to bring back the idea of 'think and act like an owner' for businesses to really understand their customer base better.[3] The ability of family businesses to leverage this entrepreneurial spark and refocus on the mission of the business remains more promising than in complex corporate organizations.

In most instances, family businesses can be classified as[4]:

- **Nuclear family business**: It usually revolves around the parents and their children. Here, succession planning and cross-generational understanding tend to be the focus issues.

- **Extended family business:** It may include uncles, aunts, in-laws, and cousins, and is likely to have been in existence for several generations before reaching its current status. Here, the key focus is usually to ensure that the family members are on the same page about collective business goals.

- **Sibling partnership**: In such a partnership, sibling dynamics and rivalries become critical concerns for the business.

- **Adoptive family business**: Based on a more liberal definition of family, adoptive family businesses incorporate those who marry into the family or even a good friend of the family.

The composition of a family business ecosystem can be complex with the immediate family, the extended one, and friends thrown into the mix. Navigating issues of seniority and the chain of command while challenging age, gender, and social norms is a common feature under this type of management. The generational gap often brings about differences in values, opinions, worldviews, and working styles. The challenge is to turn these competing forces into advantageous high-functioning cohesive actions.

International businesses often view industrial growth as capital-intensive, where increased output necessitates increased inputs such as financing, machinery, manpower, and natural resources. However, in a developing economy like India, with an acute scarcity of most of these inputs, it should come as no surprise that businesses have grown accustomed to doing more with less. Many innovations have emerged due to the scarcity of resources, not because of extensive research and development, but because necessity drives businesses to find cost-effective solutions.

Given that the Indian consumer market is rather price- and value-conscious, comprising largely of families with modest incomes, Indian businesses have developed a tendency to be highly creative in their use of resources. Operating within the confines of the red tape of complex Indian bureaucracy – made more difficult by limited resources – business owners 'have learned to rely on their wits to circumvent hurdles they recurrently confront'.[5] They have remained willing to adjust and course-correct, with an ability to accommodate extreme volatility.

When I first joined MPIL in 2008, I enrolled myself for a 'Six Sigma' certification course. Six Sigma is a management methodology designed to increase efficiency by standardizing processes, a highly effective technique that relies on repeatability and reproducibility of each process or instrument. I was keen to build my skills, particularly when it came to factory floor management. The Six Sigma technique focuses on reducing uncertainty and risk such that output is predictable, and, therefore, controllable. So, after a week-long seminar, I returned to the factory floor, excited to put my learnings to use. I reshuffled processes and operations with the help of my team and developed metrics to measure key statistics including production per machine per hour and the operators and time required by the machines to pack, load, and dispatch products. I was so determined to achieve the 99.99966 percent efficiency level of the Six Sigma methodology that I ignored the unquantifiable and qualitative aspects of the floor.

Consequently, I faced several hiccups and found myself unable to implement the standardization demanded by Six Sigma. I finally realized every single order was unique in its colour of steel, size, dispatch schedule, and payment terms. Who was I kidding? We were not an assembly line that mass-produced bottles or pens of the same size or colour. Our products were selling *because* they were custom-made; mass standardization was simply not an option for us.

Similarly, whenever a part needed to be repaired or replaced, instead of logging an official request for a replacement part as I had instructed the plant managers, my father would simply address it by welding parts together, moving things around, and pulling long cables by himself to get the machine working with minimal downtime. Nimble and thrifty, his method lends itself to success during times of crisis, since arriving at a systematic fix would have taken longer than applying the fix itself. By trying to apply standardized solutions borrowed from others to our unique establishment, we were setting ourselves up for failure.

A process-driven approach does not work in an environment of customized orders, where employees are used to pitching in whenever needed, and where disruptions often come at inopportune moments. Six Sigma attempts to institutionalize stability and predictability in a volatile, rapidly changing world with diverse customers who have specific requirements. But trying to implement a 'one size fits all' approach to our operations often ended up causing longer delays than our seemingly disorderly and reactive responses to a problem. We came up with innovative solutions for every problem we faced. Flexibility was our strength, and a system that championed rigidity and standardization would have held us back. We had got so good at 'makeshift' solutions that they had become the norm.

When manufacturing consultants from Frost & Sullivan visited our plant, they were impressed by our ability to recycle 96 percent of our scrap material. Our modest factory – full of unorthodox, cost-effective solutions – won their Green Manufacturing Excellence Award in 2010. Some of

India's most respectable organizations, including L&T and Hindustan Unilever, were among the other winners.

The same year, I attended a breakfast meet organized by the Mumbai chapter of The Indus Entrepreneurs (TiE), an entrepreneurship organization. There, I heard everyone discuss a term I had never heard before – SaaS. A kind young man next to me explained that SaaS referred to 'Software as a Service' – a cloud-based delivery model for online business applications. SaaS services can be used by SMEs for brainstorming, accounting, networking, documenting, measuring employee morale levels, and more. We soon implemented one such free tool at MPIL for intra-organizational communication to streamline our internal discussions. This led me to envision the future of our management as simple and collaborative.

The Western-style approach to innovation can at times be elitist and insular as Radjou, Prabhu, and Ahuja correctly identify in their exemplary work *Jugaad Innovation*. In the book, they challenge the assumption that top-of-the-line technology is necessary for innovation. I could not agree more. While technology and research are indeed crucial, they do not need to be expensive or exclusive. In fact, a Global Innovation 1000 study by the consulting firm Strategy& (previously Booz and Company) found no statistically significant relationship between a firm's financial performance and its spending on innovation.[6]

They also noted that companies like Apple spend less than their peers on R&D (research and development) while still outperforming them. As per this study, high-leverage innovators have a deep understanding of their end user's needs, a culture of innovation and an actively involved senior leadership. These are characteristics intrinsic to family businesses in India.

Unique solutions can emerge more easily in smaller, less hierarchical organizations, particularly ones built on strong bonds. When motivated employees brainstorm and keep tackling the problems, they can come to amazing solutions. We have no PhDs in our office; my father, of course, jokes he has a PhD in jugaad from an unknown university in Hisar, Haryana, that pushes out successful graduates year after year. Yet, somehow, our team still makes things work. Stubbornness, collaboration, and frugality can encourage managerial styles that produce creative solutions at little or no expense.

Why do Family Businesses Need to Be Reclaimed?

Offensive stereotypes likening family businesses to '*lala*' companies or '*baniye ki dukaan*' (hand-me-down mom-and-pop shops lacking sophistication and prospect) have had a damaging impact. Such negative labels lead to mental roadblocks for the Indian youth, deterring them from returning to their family businesses after their education. Family businesses are projected as hopeless entities without any room for improvement or reform; such cliches undermine the ideology and experience of first-generation business owners in the eyes of other family members.

At first, I worried about the same things at MPIL, where our way of doing things made us look exactly like a 'baniye ki dukaan'. I was wary of those who mocked such businesses that clung to reducing costs and resisting the latest business fads. When I nervously admitted this fear to my father, he said vehemently, 'You're damn right we are a lala company. But because we hound expenses and costs, we don't need to worry about profits. We are afloat in this sinking economy because we are frugal.' And just like that, my father transformed my embarrassment into empowerment.

The *baniya* (merchant) mentality can be a useful perspective in business as it provides a simple yet foolproof path to success or at least stability. Take the old joke about a baniya who dies and meets Yamraj, the Hindu god of death, who is to decide his fate in the afterlife. Yamraj asks the baniya in a thunderous voice, 'Oye Gupta, do you want to go to heaven or hell?' The baniya replies sheepishly, 'Maharaj, send me wherever there is greater margin.'

Talk to any baniya businessman and he will break down business school for you with this age-old management mantra:

Take stock of what you have in the morning. Then take stock of what you have before you leave for the evening. Subtract morning from evening. If you come up with a positive number, you are doing okay. If it's negative, something is wrong. Nothing can cushion its impact. You are doing something wrong – period.

The baniya mentality is uncomplicated: watch the costs, and profits will follow. If more businesses around the world lived by the baniya mentality, we might not have ended up with the 2008 crash. Such stereotypes must be reclaimed to make family businesses more appealing to the youth. Here, I present reasons why family businesses must be recognized as legitimate organizations at the forefront of all national policy agenda, and why business owners (and the next generation) need to reclaim their seat at the table.

Family businesses are engines of the economy

Family businesses are the underdogs of the business world and often get a bad rep because they are less publicized, less studied, and less understood (thus, often misrepresented) than their corporate counterparts. They are characterized as unprofessional, nepotistic, stagnant, and too informal, leading to an undervaluation of their true worth and contributions to the economy. Family businesses, which are typically SMEs, form the backbone of many communities – employing households, forging wide social networks, providing key local services, and launching important social initiatives.

According to the World Bank, SMEs 'represent about 90% of businesses and more than 50% of employment worldwide. Formal SMEs contribute up to 40% of national income (GDP) in emerging economies.'[7] In India, family businesses are the largest economic drivers and collective employers. They contribute to over 70 percent of the Indian GDP.[8] The PwC Family Business Survey (2012-2013) found that 78 percent of family businesses go out of their way to retain staff even in the most adverse conditions.[9] Speaking about the effect of the Covid-19 pandemic on family businesses, Devang Jhaveri, second-generation business owner of the luxury goods brand Devotie, shared with me in an interview, 'A family business has a better chance to survive and recoup as compared to a corporate structure, as family-run businesses usually do not over-trade, are not heavily debt-backed and don't over-employ.'

Governments and municipalities must take this into account to ensure that the right opportunities and incentives are in place for family businesses to thrive. So far, family businesses have been taken for granted. There is a need for a policy framework that offers recognition and respect to family businesses as a separate entity and an industry in their own right. Family businesses in India, especially the smaller ones, would benefit from easier access to low-cost finance, training and management support, centres for conflict resolution outside of the formal courts as well as an environment of stable business regulations and tax laws.

Family businesses uplift families and communities

Families are crucial for cohesive communities and help in maintaining democratic peace and nation-building. They offer key financial, emotional, and institutional support to their immediate and extended members; in the business world, this can have multi-fold benefits, including entry into various business and social networks, financing opportunities, and mentorship and guidance.

A few years ago, an Indian credit rating agency decided to downgrade our rating. While our business was doing well – both revenue and bottom line were improving – the larger industry was experiencing instability, which was perhaps the reason behind the downgrading. In a detailed email to the agency, I explained my rationale as to why our rating should not change, and if anything, should improve. They promptly expressed their disagreement, so I insisted on meeting the senior management. I tirelessly presented my case in the meeting. The directors feigned interest and made derogatory remarks about the scale of our business. Ignoring their jabs, I kept at my arguments. The rating was important for us to maintain credibility with our bankers.

Then suddenly, my father, who had been quiet the entire time, had had enough. Surprising us all, he banged both his fists on the table, accused the directors of complacency, and insisted that the meeting was over.

I was red with embarrassment. My dad walked out, and I followed him. In the car, I unloaded my frustration at his behaviour. 'Why did you have to do that? Now there is no way our rating will be reconsidered!' He replied sternly, 'I was angry that they were making you work so hard for it. You had to talk so much. And they did not seem to appreciate it. I didn't want to waste your energy over such nincompoops. You are too smart for them. We have a good track record and relationship with our bankers. We will manage.'

My father was unnerved that I was being treated unfairly, and thus he chose to protect me over our business. In his view, the business could be managed, but family always came first.

As luck would it, his theatrics worked. The directors authorized a second inquiry into our business and our previous year's rating was retained. It was a small mercy in the grand scheme of things, but it led me to think about how family business founders define their priorities. When I shared my story with other friends with their own family businesses, they responded with a flood of anecdotes about instances where seemingly illogical decisions had been made to protect the interests of the family. My father was right; if our family was fine, we could deal with any situation at work. I have now come to believe that as long as the 'family' in 'family business' comes first, we will be okay.

Family businesses preserve history and legacy

Family businesses are excellent vehicles for intergenerational knowledge transfers. The dynamics of a family business across generations unleash valuable social capital, promotes experiential learning, passes down best practices (via anecdotes, norms, values, and operating procedures), and shapes local and regional histories. They are naturally prone to thinking in generational terms and focus on strengthening familial bonds and community-building. The family business format has survived the British Raj and post-Independence reforms, and has grown in the face of international competition after the 1990 economic policies were implemented. This makes family businesses not just crucial for the long-term development of our country, but also for carrying forward our core values, our cultural heritage, and the very Indian spirit to excel against all odds.

Family businesses amplify learning

In small family businesses, employees wear several hats, given the limitations of resources and pressures of time, which results in magnified on-the-job learning and personal development. Within their intimate set-up, family businesses are also more conducive to promoting employees' professional development, given the personal bonds formed at all levels of the workforce. There is a huge emphasis on emotional learning and appreciation for a personalized take on business and work ethics. Many a times, a system running on trust and relationship may prove to be more foolproof than modern channels of due diligence.

Family businesses provide stability

In the aftermath of the 2008 economic collapse, family businesses saw a resurgence. A study conducted by Credit Suisse in 2018 found that after an initial dip in performance in 2008, family-owned companies have consistently outperformed non-family-owned businesses year on year.[10] And within family businesses, small-capital businesses have grown much faster than large-cap ones. This resurgence is largely due to their inherent focus on long-term revenue growth and reliance on organic cash flow to fund innovation, along with a preference for conservative funding structures. As per a 2019 PwC report, family businesses, owing to their outlook of measuring success over generations, were found to be more resilient to economic ups and downs.[11] They offer more consistency and stability than corporate-managed affairs because, as mentioned earlier, they are more risk-averse, frugal, and innovative in the ways in which they operate. As such, they become more resistant to economic shifts.

This could be seen during the Covid-19 pandemic as well when family businesses around the world devised creative solutions to respond to the challenges around them. Serum Institute, founded by Cyrus Poonawalla, now under the leadership of his son Adar Poonawalla, was the first organization to come up with a vaccine for the coronavirus in India.[12] Anticipating the demand for masks when the pandemic struck India, Anita Dongre, leading fashion designer, and her son Yash Dongre, Business Head for House of Anita Dongre, began producing face masks at their rural production centres.[13]

Family businesses act as launch pads for entrepreneurs

Family businesses are ideal settings for those new to the entrepreneurial world to get their feet wet, given the support network such a business provides. The innovative and startup atmosphere of a family business helps develop skills in creative problem-solving, conflict resolution, multitasking, and stakeholder engagement. The pace of change, with the new generation entering the family business, has seen tremendous improvement from fifty to sixty years to under ten years because the younger generation is much more adept at incorporating technology.[14] Many of these businesses have expanded to new industries, offering family members a chance to experiment, learn, and become experts in these new areas quickly. Take, for instance, Mudit Mohini, a third-generation family business leader of the beloved Delhi Press Group (of *Champak* and *Grihshobha* fame), who led the initiative to take her business from traditional publishing to digital publishing and create an online learning management system. This ensured that they remained relevant in the world of quick 'Whatsapp reading' and, at the same time, were able to expand into the school and student market.

Family businesses are social change-makers

One of the biggest strengths of Indian business families is their understanding of their immediate environment. Given how embedded family businesses are within their communities, they have significant influence over the people and the environment around them. This connection, which sometimes lasts for generations, is difficult for the corporate world to replicate. Family businesses that get involved in charity, philanthropy (for instance, in the arts or education), environmental sustainability, and other causes, inspire communities to create change in meaningful and impactful ways. JSW Foundation, part of the multibillion-dollar JSW Group, with interests in steel, power, energy, and cement, has single-handedly restored and transformed the historic town of Hampi in Karnataka. JSW Shakti, an initiative by the same group, strives to empower women through sustainable employment and has set up several internationally recognized BPO (business process outsourcing) centres.

Family businesses offer a fallback option

A 2019 study published by PwC shows that 73 percent of the next-gen members of family businesses in India work for these businesses.[15] Generation Y and Z are keen to protect and grow the family wealth. They are driven by the scope for greater empowerment and purpose offered by the family business.

Moreover, the job market is fiercely competitive and recent graduates must excel more and more to outshine their peers and secure employment. Though no less competitive, family businesses have provided a respectable, convenient and readily available avenue for the current generation, and will do so for those to come, especially in the face of international economic crises like the Covid-19 pandemic. A family business is a safety net, an admirable fallback option for many young people entering the job market.

During my research, I met with Saahil Sethu, a young, dynamic aerospace engineer who trained in the US. The restraints on H1-B visas and the high unemployment rates in the US while the Covid-19 pandemic was at its peak left him with no choice but to return home to Aurangabad. He joined his father's polymers-trading business. When I spoke with him, he described his employment in the family business, which had never been his first choice, as: 'It is good enough and good enough is just fine.' He said he had turned down many opportunities because they hadn't seemed 'good enough', but in the urgency of the moment and his prolonged unemployed state, he had come to accept and appreciate a role for himself in his father's business. Now he cannot imagine himself anywhere else but right there by his father's side, growing their business. After speaking to Saahil, I realized that in difficult and uncertain times, having a fallback option in one's family business is a valuable resource.

Family businesses are crucial for gender equality

Family businesses, by their very nature, have allowed women freedom, flexibility, and job security.[16] Women have always been involved in running family businesses, whether their contribution has been formally recognized or not. Women, directly or indirectly involved in a family business, have worked from home long before WFH became a widely recognized acronym during the pandemic. Their dual loyalty to both the family and the business enables them to provide support at home and work, solve problems, and hold the family together. The power and influence they have over the family business make them an essential part of the management team.[17] Therefore, family businesses can and have served as a starting point for achieving gender equality.

My friend Samar has been a pathbreaker in the manufacturing industry, leading her family business alongside other family members. Our discussions about our active involvement in our respective businesses have always been animated, as we fire away comparisons, generalizations, and analyses. Out of our conversations emerged an awareness of the sheer variety of avenues and opportunities that a family business can offer the women in the family. It is almost as though women can find a role suited to their individual personality.

For example, there could be leadership roles for those interested in management positions, or flexible consultant roles for those who want to be brought in as and when needed, or independent departments within the business for those who want to be in charge. One daughter may be more extroverted and pursue a sales director type of public role. Another daughter within the same family may be introverted and prefer a more private, behind-the-scenes type of position, like managing the warehouse. It is understood that if mothers want to come and work in the office, there would be no barrier to their entry. It is not just because they know more than anyone else about the business, but also because there is always something that they could do for the business to increase its value. Their contribution would be appreciated and helpful. A family business is always open to women, offering a unique platform that they would not otherwise have in a corporate structure.

Women's continuous involvement in family businesses has also facilitated greater awareness of their role in society among the men around them. Even the most confident of women benefit from an external support network. Continuous reassurance from the family can help women feel comfortable pursuing opportunities outside their homes. Men in family businesses who value equality can help women by challenging the archaic and misogynistic opinions of other men. For instance, when fathers bring their daughters to meetings outside the office, they help knock down barriers for other women.

A qualitative study conducted by Kim Harland (in which I participated as well) lays out that family businesses around the world fare much better than corporates in their contribution towards gender diversity and equity.[18] The goal to preserve and help a business flourish through multiple generations requires that the family also remain cohesive and content. Hence, the involvement of both men and women in the family is essential, much more so than in an individual-centric corporation where there is an emphasis on personal benefit and pressure to showcase individual performance. Interviews featured in Harland's book highlight narratives of women from around the world about how they have thrived in the businesses run by their families.

Why are family businesses more likely to back women? Ernst & Young's 2019 Family Business Report found the primary reasons to be that women have a long-term mindset, are able to create an inclusive environment at work as they would do at home and are more influential as role models.[19] Particularly in India, we have seen better results with the increasing participation of women in their family business.[20] With shrinking family size and improvement in women's access to education, their participation within the business has become easier. According to research conducted at the Indian School of Business, the amendment of the Hindu Succession Act in 2005 also facilitated the same by allowing daughters or female family members to be equal heirs of the family business.[21]

Out of the many formal interviews with women in family businesses that inform this book, one account touched me in particular because of how meaningful the family business platform has been for the interviewee. Surbhi, a strong, independent woman obtained an MBA from Symbiosis Institute of Management in Pune. She did not like the idea of joining her father's business, a wholesale textile shop in Kalbadevi, a busy commercial district in South Bombay. Also, the business was rather old school and the market itself was all-male. So, she joined a human resources recruitment company, where she met someone, who she went on to marry. Unfortunately, Surbhi's marriage with this man did not work out, and she eventually divorced him.

Soon after her divorce, as though things in her life were not hard enough, Surbhi faced significant backlash at work. Colleagues were judgmental and would break into gossip upon seeing her. This further crushed her confidence, as she felt like a pariah almost everywhere she went. She said that during those difficult times she received strength and support from her parents. She quit her job and moved back in with them to heal emotionally under her mother's care.

One day at dinner, her father said out of the blue that he wanted to make a suggestion. He seemed quite hesitant and the first thought that came to Surbhi's mind was that he might ask her to give meeting someone new another shot. She felt her body tense up, but nonetheless, listened carefully.

'I was thinking sitting at home must be boring for you. You are not the type of person who likes to be at indoors. And I know I don't have much to offer in terms of a career, but the shop could use some help, even if you feel like coming only for a few hours daily. It will freshen your mind. What do you say?'

What could she say? She was so touched by her father's gesture that she said yes, instantly. She saw her father's shop in an entirely new light. It wasn't fancy, but it had good volumes in sales. Business was done in informal yet effective ways: men came in, had discussions, and placed their orders. She felt much more welcome here as she took on responsibilities at the shop, building connections and rapport with the clients. They became so comfortable with conversing with her that often those men would beg her to marry their sons!

Surbhi could not believe that only a few years ago she had dismissed her own family business, only to find immense support and self-confidence in this informal, unglamorous shop, among men of her father's age who accepted her wonderfully. Surbhi has been working at her father's shop for four years now. Happy and content with her life, she now enjoys baking and travelling in her free time and brings her parents along whenever she can.

For me, my brother and father have been my biggest champions in the office, calling out instances of misogynist behaviour every time it occurred. It was because of my brother's encouragement that my mother learned to drive, swim, and travel by herself, all after the age of forty. I once asked my father how he felt about working with me. He replied how he had been warned repeatedly (by his supposed well-wishers) that by educating me and allowing me to work, he was significantly reducing my chances of an arranged marriage. Although he had been anxious after seeing me thrive at the workplace – knowing it too well that it would be difficult to find an Indian family that accepted an ambitious *bahu* – he believed in my potential and couldn't get himself to pay further attention to these external voices.

I have seen first-hand how such support can encourage women. That is why I believe all young women must first tap into their own family networks to succeed at their workplaces. Often, family members do not get the credit they deserve for their contributions towards gender equality. Having said that, there is tremendous work ahead of us in ensuring that women in family businesses are better recognized and supported.

3

RECLAIMING FAMILY BUSINESSES

NOW THAT WE KNOW WHY FAMILY BUSINESSES ARE important, how do we go about bringing them back at the forefront of all economic discussions? In this section, I discuss ten oft-quoted stereotypes about family businesses and ways to reinterpret them for their benefit. This is a great starting point to reset the conversation and give them the recognition they deserve.

Why Family Businesses Matter and How to Reclaim Them

Common Stereotypes	Ground Reality
1. Lala company or mom and pop shop	Mom and pop know best
2. Too small to matter	Small but mighty
3. Offer limited opportunities to employees	Offer longevity and security to employees

Common Stereotypes	Ground Reality
4. Bring no new perspective	Get behind new ideas collectively
5. Facilitate top-down decision-making	Utilize the trickle-up approach
6. Marred by nepotism	Nurture the 'professional nepot'
7. Too personal or emotional	Draw energy from the personal
8. Unprofessional and un-corporate	Blend the corporate and the informal
9. Closed off	Embrace the next gen
10. Keep out the in-laws	Tie in the extended family

1. Mom and pop know best

Family businesses are often criticized for being lala companies and mom-and-pop businesses for their supposed lack of sophistication and seemingly simple business methods. But what some see as rudimentary business practices can in fact be viewed as frugality, innovation, and astuteness from a different perspective. A research study by Alvarez & Marsal on small family business shows that they greatly benefit from a single founder or promoter who offers quick decision-making and agility.[1] Such small businesses often have limited products/services and an established customer base which they understand very well. Moreover, the cohesion between family members and their business responsibilities results in a lean and cost-effective structure.

Instead of comparing their structure, or growth, vis-à-vis larger corporate competitors, family businesses must measure themselves against internal parameters such as longevity of the business, improvement in the lifestyle of family members, and the growth of their employees. To appreciate family businesses, there is a need to embrace the hustle and creativity that enables them to succeed. Smaller businesses offer multi-dimensional – professional, personal, and familial – fulfilment, something many corporates cannot. Managers and workers within these organizations see their jobs as much more than the source of their livelihood, but as a vehicle for their advancement and stability. They pour in their heart and soul into keeping the business going, because of how interconnected their lives become.

The best way to overcome stereotypical perceptions is to stop worrying about them, and instead start recognizing your firm's strengths and make them work for you. Family businesses, especially in India, are often viewed as unprofessional and outdated models. There are certainly examples of the above, but on the whole, family businesses demonstrate far more responsibility and accountability towards their businesses and their customers, given the stakes attached to the business as well as the family's reputation. Sumant Batra, a corporate and policy lawyer, has investigated how image-conscious family businesses are.[2] He finds that family members involved in the business see their enterprise as a part of their identity and source of their social bonds. Doing right by all the stakeholders is, therefore, linked to their image and social standing.

Family businesses are also said to be unsystematic in their approach to operations; in other words, they are said to conduct business haphazardly. When compared to larger organizations, a small or medium-sized family firm is less likely to have specific policies in place, but that does not mean they are unprofessional. In fact, because the stakes for the owner are incredibly high – the business, after all, represents their livelihood, reputation, and legacy – there is added pressure on the owner to act in an organized, thoughtful, and responsible manner. Their less rigid approach can also be a boon to those who work with them. Because the 'top boss' is directly involved, decisions can be made quickly as negotiations do not require countless approvals. These firms do not face as much red tape as larger corporate entities and work closely with clients and stakeholders to get to the bottom of issues quickly. Their 'unconventional' approach to business is simply an innovation in the face of limited resources. Such creativity should be celebrated, not condemned.

Here, I want to share the example of my high school friend Gaurav, who was bullied at school because his father owned a plumbing and sanitation business. Although Gaurav never let on in school, he was embarrassed by his father's business because it seemed so unglamorous and dirty. To his horror, someone found out that his father dealt with pipes, drains, and fittings, and began calling him *kachrawala* (garbage man). Years later, Gaurav and I reconnected, thanks to Facebook, and met for dinner. He had become a chartered accountant and told me that he was so put off by years of hiding the truth about his dad's business that he wanted to pursue a different profession. However, he would help his father out with tax and accounting matters and remained, albeit privately, impressed with how successful the business was. His father was brilliant at what he did and had branched out into luxury fittings and turnkey design solutions. After a few years of working as an accountant, Gaurav eventually joined his father's business. He has not looked back since. His business had taken him to Italy and Mexico, from where they imported high-end materials. His eyes lit up when he spoke about their future plans. If anyone called him a kachrawala today, he said, he would smile, knowing well how rewarding it was to be one.

2. Small but mighty

Family businesses are often criticized for counting every single penny to the point of appearing stingy or particularly tight-fisted (in other words, a baniye ki dukaan). But what is there to be ashamed of in trying to control costs? Family businesses should flip the script more often and recognize that their cost-consciousness allows them to do more with less. Frugality does not necessarily mean stinginess. It is precisely this attention to cost that can help small businesses survive in times of an economic downturn. Since 2006, small family businesses have consistently performed better in terms of revenue growth than large businesses.[3] Small size does not impact sustainability; small businesses do not need to become big to survive.

A family business's continual focus on frugality means it does not need to operate in extremes; it remains steady, thanks to smart financial practices. This is not to say that they do not invest in the future. Since the business has been passed down to them, the owners are often more willing to spend for a greater gain in the long term. Immediate profits do not drive the business as much as its long-term health. Furthermore, by instilling cost-consciousness as a core value, family members develop shrewd negotiation skills. Simply put, they are unwilling to accept a less profitable deal if there is even the slightest chance of getting a better one.

Family businesses also must begin to emphasize the truth that 'small is the new big'. This is best described in the following anecdote: A friend – let's call him Mr Srinivas – encouraged my father to go to Kuala Lumpur to meet the owner of his multinational corporation with an impeccable reputation in the steel construction industry. My father, determined to run with the lead, informed us he was going to Malaysia that very weekend to meet the owner, Mr A. N. We thought our father was crazy to go on a fool's errand. But sure enough, he met A. N. at a cafe on a Sunday. A. N. shared with my father his personal growth story and his experiences building a large business from scratch. A. N.'s business was family-run too, and they valued quality and trust among their suppliers. He was proud of how lean and cost-efficient his factories were.

My father laid all his cards on the table – that we had the infrastructure at our plants but not enough work, and that we had limited technical knowhow. But at the same time, our plant was a malleable space that could be transformed to suit any project's requirement. A. N. and my father must have had quite a meeting for it ran longer than planned, and A. N. drove my father to the airport for his flight back to Mumbai.

Today, we've been working with A. N. for over a decade. We manufactured the primary steel structure for Mumbai's international airport's Terminal 2 together at our factory. Perhaps A. N. saw in my father a driven business owner who was willing to learn and put in the hard work. He trusted my father to be involved himself, to watch the costs, and to take responsibility. So, when A. N. needed an Indian partner, he chose my father. Companies larger than us and with more experience wondered how we could bring in such a large player as a technical collaborator. But we knew that our flexibility, our frugality, and our direct involvement had given us an edge over them. We were humble, honest, and hardworking, and that was more than many in our industry could claim about themselves.

Steel columns at Chhatrapati Shivaji Maharaj International Airport, Mumbai, made at our factory

3. Offer longevity and security to employees

It may look like family businesses only care about developing the careers of key family members and not as much about the other employees that make the business run. They can sometimes struggle to attract talent, due to perceptions that they do not allow employees any opportunity for career growth.

Family businesses need to counter such negative perceptions by making it clear that not only do they provide opportunities to all employees, but that they can also do so on a multigenerational basis which helps strengthen community bonds in the long term. Growth opportunities can often be incredible due to the startup nature of many such firms. Further, because of the more flexible and intimate structure of family businesses, they often allow advancement within the organization at a faster pace, and talent is often recognized far more quickly. Moreover, family businesses tend to have stronger connections with their employees, which means they are more likely to provide training and development that allow employees to grow their potential further. In *The India Way*, the authors shed light on how this culture of family among the workforce – taking care of the staff and providing them with resources to take on independent decisions – has been reciprocated by employees in the form of commitment, trust, and hard work.[4]

Employees are the ultimate armour of a business. When an employee's family members also enter the same business, it strengthens the network even more. One of the most beautiful things about family businesses is that they are a mesh of many families woven together. The trust and comfort are often palpable. From our office to our factories, we have employees whose spouses and even children work with us. My grandfather, for example, was a contractor for another family business in Hisar, Haryana. My father has undertaken many construction and logistics projects for the same man's son for many decades. Today, my brother and I continue to receive orders from the same business, now being led by the grandson of the founder. Essentially, three generations of my family have worked with three generations of another.

4. Get behind new ideas collectively

A family business is usually managed by its members, who are said to be steeped in decades of tradition, thus creating the perception that such firms possess an immutable culture that lacks newer perspectives. However, this does not have to be the case. While family businesses may be more reserved when faced with new ideas due to being risk-averse, such a layer of caution can actually be a boon. Because, instead of chasing trends, such firms tend to focus on core competencies and strengths. They are willing to consider new perspectives, but only if they enhance existing strengths. Several such examples suggest family businesses can integrate fresh concepts of marketing, online distribution, and logistics quite easily.

One such example is the Nalli Group of Companies. In a 2016 Forbes profile, Ramanathan Nalli, vice chairperson of the group, recounted how his daughter Lavanya Nalli (also a vice chairperson at the company) brought in 'a system, rigour and discipline' and plans to launch a 'new ecommerce platform' as well as 'customer-relationship and business-intelligence systems'.[5] At the young age of thirty-five she had injected a fresh perspective into a ninety-year-old family business.

Rather than being stagnant, because new generations of family members constantly join the business, the 'clan-like' structure allows for greater acceptance of new ideas. Such businesses build strong relationships with their customers and suppliers and this familiarity creates a 'comfort zone' that allows for greater consideration and acceptance of new ideas. There are many examples of family businesses adopting fresh ideas around us. Kishore Biyani, founder and CEO of Future Group, has built a successful business over the last couple of decades. We are all familiar with the Big Bazaar retail stores and what a breakthrough they had been for the Indian retail experience. Leveraging her father's generation's stronghold in the retail marketplace, Avni Biyani conceptualized and established the gourmet grocery store Foodhall in 2011.

But such ideas are not just limited to big business. Our neighbours, the Bhargavas, in suburban Mumbai, a fun-loving Gujarati family, have owned a photo studio for over three decades. However, despite the rapid evolution in photo-editing technology and digital printing, Mr Bhargava's store continues to find new ways to print, design, edit, and create. This is made possible by the fresh energy constantly infused by his pioneering daughter Himani, who joined the business after completing her higher education. She is the perfect bridge between her father, the employees, and new-age customers. You will come across many such businesses which accommodate new methods within traditional set-ups in their own *jugaadu* way if you were to take a walk down your street.

5. Utilize the trickle-up approach

The stereotype that only patriarchs or matriarchs are responsible for success in family businesses is far from the truth. Employees at all levels are involved in decision-making in the most successful family businesses, giving them the chance to learn through experience, exposure, rotations, trust, faith, and, most importantly, by being able to use their voice. While it may appear that instructions flow from the top to the bottom, ideas and thoughts informing those decisions in fact move upwards.

Moreover, the employees often need to juggle diverse roles to respond to the changing needs of family businesses, and therefore, the senior management has to be open to their inputs and views. In the most successful family businesses, employees are considered to be family members. This helps them feel empowered and connected to their work. Such an attitude also helps foster informal support networks and build a sense of community and security, resulting in greater employee trust and satisfaction.

Because of the owner's active presence, family businesses are accused of micromanaging their employees and lacking autonomy. This is, however, a fundamental misunderstanding of the relationship between employees and owners of a family business. When employees are genuinely treated as an extension of the family, there is greater access to the owner, and therefore, requests and suggestions can be conveyed more easily. The personal nature of this relationship means that the owners also desire greater employee development. There is a real sense of pride in helping them move up the career ladder to allow them to contribute greatly to the organization.

Family businesses tend to reward employees who can troubleshoot independently. With loose structures in place, employees can experiment to arrive at solutions. And sometimes, because of the culture of doing more with less and troubleshooting, family businesses also create 'intrapreneurs'.

Roma Bakshani, a second-generation family business owner, is the director of BNT Connections, a garment-manufacturing house based in Tamil Nadu and Kerala with woven and knit divisions supplying garments to large international brands such as New Balance and Umbro. Roma shared with me how her father, Mr J. Thakur Bakshani, founder of the business, had his main 'fabric man' Sethu start the knit division of their business in Tirupur. Sethu was an immensely knowledgeable and hard-working team member, considered to be a 'second brother' by Roma's father. Sethu's creativity, love for fabrics and knitting, along with the backing and support of Roma's father, gave him the confidence to run with this new venture and make it successful. Today, Sethu's daughter Shrutika also works in the business. Roma explained to me that sometimes as family members in business together, we are more emotional towards our brothers or nephews and can be much more objective in our dealings with employees. Sethu's example and intrapreneurial venture is an inspiring story of an employee's close bond with the owner, as well as of an owner's faith and trust in their key team members.

In my father's case, Raghuram, who has worked with my father since he was twenty-one – now forty-five – is one such intrapreneur. He first assisted my father with his transport business, managing the loading, unloading, and billing of trucks. He gradually emerged as a natural 'fixer', or expediter of sorts who dealt with issues and delays, thereby reducing my father's direct involvement. Today, he runs several project sites by himself, some of which my father has not even visited. For my father, assigning a task to Raghuram means the work will get done.

6. Nurture the 'professional nepot'

Nepotism is a frequent charge against family businesses; after all, the business is passed down from generation to generation. Some see this as a negative aspect of family businesses, claiming family members are given undeserved roles. Outsiders believe family members receive undeserved promotions and perks while other employees get left behind. Central to this claim is that the family member is preferred over a non-family member, *without regard for merit.* Nepotism need not be an inherently negative practice. If you have been grooming your child to perform a vital role within your organization, they may be a perfect fit and bring a wealth of intellectual capital. Or it could be so that your child may have no interest in the business, in which case, you would be better off hiring someone more qualified.

It is only natural that the children of the leaders will be groomed for future leadership positions. For the most part, the next-generation family members are trained and prepared for it throughout their lives. They draw strength and purpose from the family unit, enabling them to perform better at work. They are privy to the historical context of many key decisions of the business and have witnessed several milestones first-hand. It is thus a generalization to claim managerial roles are handed over to the undeserving. In reality, the younger generation cannot skate by without making the effort. Given the intimacy within a family business, their non-performance becomes obvious to all, and the constant vigilance which their performance is subjected to necessitates they need to shine before moving up the ladder. Considering how important the business is to the founder, a move to hand it over to someone incapable of managing the responsibility could put their entire legacy at risk.

John Davis, professor and founder of Harvard's Family Business Management Studies, talks of a 'professional nepot' – a family member equipped with the right 'package' of capabilities, experiences, and values to run the family business as a professional organization.[6] As per Davis, often is the case that family members have an advantage over external employees, especially when it comes to dealing with shareholders, customers, and suppliers. Davis rightly states that it is important to challenge those who imply that the only way to be 'professional' is to be 'non-family'. Family members can instil specific confidence about the stability and perseverance of a company among all stakeholders. We must not fall into the trap of thinking that to make a business more 'professional' it needs to be rid of family members. It may come to that in some cases for sure, but it cannot be the assumption we start with.

The founder needs to work hard and create a better version of themselves in their children. When you see a doctor look at her toddler playing with a toy doctor set, you know she is thinking about what a great doctor her child will make. The doctor passes on nuanced information to the child during their interactions without even thinking about it. The child picks up more and more each time she visits mom's clinic. Twenty years later, if she gives her daughter an internship at her clinic, should it be called nepotism? This is the moment the doctor would have wished for herself and her child – to work together. And quite honestly, there are advantages to working with someone from your family – the familial shorthand makes things easier. You don't have to constantly explain the details or act as a tour guide at the organization since a family member's familiarity with the basic context can be taken for granted. In the next chapter, I will illustrate how an understanding honed by decades of apprenticeship under the founder creates the best next-gen business leaders.

7. Draw energy from the personal

The idea of a family business immediately conjures up images of family feuds and in-fighting – a hotbed of soap opera drama, but with a twist of business. Given the small degree of separation between the personal and the professional in such businesses, it is no surprise that outsiders believe this would automatically lead to conflict. But, in reality, family members are perfectly capable of behaving professionally despite their personal issues. In fact, the presence of family can be a significant boon for problem-solving when conflict does arise. Because family members feel more comfortable with one another, they can develop better mediation skills that help resolve conflicts quickly and smoothly.

Some family businesses develop a reputation as gossip dens. But the flow of information in a family business does not necessarily need to be negative or harmful. In fact, by drawing on the knowledge and experience of family members, one can aggregate a wealth of information that could be useful to the business. Both community and family 'intelligence' are critical for such businesses, but this requires opening up at home and within the community.

Family businesses, like all businesses, can be rife with conflict and challenges. Often, such conflicts are grounded in personal anxieties or deep-rooted fears. Personally, my anxieties stemmed from fears of screwing up, letting my father down, and worst of all, ruining my family's business prospects. I was also anxious about how I would be perceived in a largely conservative Indian society – men my age might find me intimidating, and love or marriage might take me away from the business. Such anxieties would reveal themselves, particularly during business-related arguments. Thankfully, in my case, my mother offered a platform for free mediation. She was our sounding board, non-judgmental and fair (albeit with the occasional dramatic flair), and usually managed to get us out of our emotional cul-de-sacs. Personal feelings make us who we are; we cannot simply leave them at the door and enter a workplace. Rather, we should draw our motivation and energy from what drives, influences, and shapes us.

Each family has different patterns of conflict, but every family can find a system that works for them as long as everyone is willing. Business is personal for everyone, and it is more so in a family-owned enterprise. Instead of trying to leave behind the personal at home, it is more productive to own the personal and work with it.

8. Blend the corporate and the informal

Family businesses have navigated their progress to a modern way of doing things with great finesse. They have held their value system close and ventured out to embrace the best of what new technology has to offer. Further, the use of jugaad-inspired practices, an old-school approach to creating something new with existing resources, is an essential part of such businesses. Modern-day family businesses routinely blur the line between the old and the new to discover and create innovative ways to advance their business.

Instead of lamenting the lack of corporate tools, technology, or data-driven approaches, consider the diversity and wealth of knowledge and experience that is at your disposal. While a quantitative approach to business is essential, family businesses often thrive because of the emotional intelligence each member brings to the table and the 'street smarts' they develop along the way. Working in a family business is different from working for a big multinational, but this is not necessarily a bad thing. Family businesses tend to be more hands-on and follow a flexible and adaptable approach to business. For an employee who loves to roll their sleeves up and craves the independence to tailor different approaches to different situations, a family-run business will be the perfect fit.

For next-generation leaders, their priorities are shaped by years of experience, intuition, and knowledge that will likely lead the business to success. Mudit Mohini, director of Delhi Press, realized her passion was to spread reading and education to different parts of India. She strongly believed that each child deserves a book, a book that has quality content at a reasonable price. That's what led her to expand Delhi Press's core business of magazines and venture into books.

9. Embrace the next gen

There is a perception among the younger generation that family businesses can be intimidating – whether out of doubts that they can handle both personal and professional pressures or fears of how their relationships with other family members will be affected, or whether their voices will be heard by their parents. Others worry about the lack of formal training as they move through their careers and that they might be stuck in the family firm for life.

Family businesses, however, provide excellent opportunities to build bridges across generations. The current leaders of such a business must recognize the value younger generations bring to it, while the younger generation must recognize the learning opportunities that await them. The younger generation should be brought into the loop at a young age at lower positions instead as a direct replacement at the top. Businesses can also create some distance between family members by not making the younger ones report directly to the older ones at the workplace. The older generation should certainly make sure that their family members feel heard, and if the latter ultimately do not want a part in the business, allow them to go their own ways.

Sometimes the senior leadership might be hesitant to hand over the reins to the younger lot. They may fret over a host of questions: *Can the next generation bring their full potential to the business? Or will they ruin it and drive it to the ground? Will it result in a huge financial loss? How do I manage their egos and high expectations? Will they be able to adjust culturally? Can they follow my vision and promote our values? Are they smart, capable, and tough enough yet?*

Indeed, the questions are endless. With a solid foundation and a system of stewardship in place, business leaders can engineer an effective succession plan. It will be up to the upcoming generation to decide the business's next steps. Of course, they have to be prepared for what lies ahead, which can be done via mentoring sessions, research, courses and seminars, reviewing budgets, tapping into existing networks, and even working as interns before joining the business. Next-generation leaders should aim low and start slow, prove their worth, be patient, and show up. A successful handover requires two sides that are equally committed to the success and future of the firm.

The challenges and situations the next generation faces in their professional careers are diverse. They need to be ready for anything – from mood swings to intergenerational conflicts, from failed negotiations to bad bets. Businesses are unpredictable and dynamic, and one must hone their 'soft' skills even more to navigate this ever-changing world. The younger generation needs to learn how to convince and seek buy-ins; demonstrate leadership skills; develop business acumen; listen and empathize with others; learn to solve problems and multitask; hone social skills and discover humility; and communicate clearly. Perhaps, by excelling in these areas, they may even find their true calling. More and more, these skills – especially the soft ones that help foster human connections – are being lost or deprioritized. As generations Y and Z increasingly live and operate in digital worlds, it can be hard to develop empathy towards others. A family business environment can be the perfect place to develop these skills, especially when the leader is open to providing such opportunities to their successors.

10. Tie in the extended family

In-laws are a crucial part of the equation in family businesses and bring an entirely different flavour to the mix, either directly or indirectly. The level of their involvement may vary, but their support can be a game changer for the business, in both positive and negative ways. For example, a daughter-in-law may only be able to join her husband's business after a buy-in. The mother-in-law may entirely forbid the daughter-in-law from working or step up and be the caregiver for the grandchild while the daughter-in-law works. Therefore, the in-laws have great authority within the family, and it is best to identify how to effectively work with them to ensure a smooth relationship. Even if the in-laws are prying, over-involved, or simply difficult, the relationship does not have to be marred. By establishing clear boundaries between work and home, and putting things in writing, married couples have been able to build a positive professional rapport with their in-laws.

Delhi Press's Mudit Mohini continues to run her father's family business while being married into another family. Smita Jatia, the daughter-in-law of the Jatia family, has achieved great success for the McDonald's chain in western and southern India. She credits her success, as she took on the challenges of being a mother and a business owner, to the 'support of my husband, my in-laws, and the entire family'.[7]

A personal example would be my American in-laws. Though they belong to an entirely different culture, they are quite similar to my Indian parents: super supportive and up for the challenge. I had realized this during the early months of my marriage when my in-laws came along with me to our factory. On the long car ride back, I was on the phone with a potential client trying to make a pitch for a future order and why we were best equipped to supply a particular steel structure. When I got off the phone, my father-in-law said, 'Pri, why don't you invite the client to see the solar C-purlin that we saw on your factory floor today?' It was a terrific idea! Seeing our deliverables in person would build tremendous confidence in the client. I called the client back and offered to bring them to our factory to show them another similar structure under production and they agreed. Ultimately, I bagged that order and discovered a valuable marketing technique, thanks to my in-laws. They have been amazing sounding boards whenever I have had an issue at work, patiently analyzing the situation with me, brainstorming, and offering valuable advice.

It is evident that those involved with family businesses have to juggle between their roles at home and work. This is especially true for a daughter-in-law in the Indian context, generally speaking. In her case, the in-laws can be of invaluable help and allow her to perform her best.

With this appreciation of the complexities of family businesses and their regular championing of unique challenges, we delve into what constitutes the ultimate guide for a family business and how we can use a figurative toolkit to achieve a fulfilling career within a family enterprise and help it thrive, even in times of crisis.

4

THE ULTIMATE FAMILY BUSINESS SURVIVAL KIT

MY FATHER IS NEITHER A GRADUATE OF AN ENGINEERING college or business school nor has he worked with any other organization besides his own business. But over the course of his career, he has been a civil and mechanical engineer, an electrician, a mason, a plumber, and an artisan. No one told him what he could be; instead, he has taken his life into his own hands and crafted his future all by himself. My father has been an entrepreneur, a fixer, a hustler, a management guru, a business consultant, an opportunist, a leader, an orator, but perhaps most importantly, a believer. One would think he would be exhausted after wearing so many hats, but he continues to have incredible energy and vitality, in part due to the new challenges that come from his different roles. Not to mention, he graduated from perhaps one of the most challenging and grittiest institutions of them all: the university of life.

His professional career has taught me an invaluable lesson: the learning derived from an alternative path can sometimes trump the education received from traditional institutions. The typically passive, classroom-based learning can be of no match for the dynamic, agile, and challenging environment one finds on the job. Such has been the experience of Dr Subhash Chandra of the Zee TV Group, who joined his family business of trading after dropping out from the tenth standard, only to build one of the largest media empires in India. Even Mr Azim Premji, former Chairman of Wipro, had to leave his education at Stanford midway to take over the business when his father passed away. Today, he is known as the Czar of the Indian IT industry.

Self-taught and self-made, my father started several business ventures from scratch. These businesses were primarily based in the southern Indian states of Karnataka and Andhra Pradesh, where the language and culture barriers posed a significant challenge to a Hindi-speaking north Indian man like my father. In building his business, my father embraced south Indian food, ate the daily 'tiffin' like the locals and picked up the Kannada language. The success of these businesses not only transformed our family's life but has also been instrumental in lifting up the families of our team members. My father has always taken care of his staff members when they have been unwell or dealing with a personal problem. He has helped the children of his employees get admission into the best possible schools and colleges, and we have, as a family, attended the weddings of our employees. My father has earned the trust and respect of his stakeholders such that he has established a brand for himself, a brand that assures his customers that their projects will be completed against all odds when Ashwani Gupta is executing them. Given all that he has accomplished during his long career, it is no surprise that my father likes to remind us – with a grin – that he graduated after pursuing a forty-year-long PhD in jugaad.

Family businesses are not necessarily just about economical and quick fixes. They are primarily about presence of mind, about thinking astutely and with agility, and utilizing the resources available in the moment. For those of us in such a business, we are constantly required to adjust our ideas of what is possible, our limitations, and our capabilities.

The survival kit I discuss in this chapter teaches us to focus on the end results, instead of the ways to achieve one's goals. One needs to tap into basic human survival instincts – reach out to others for help, act speedily in the face of urgency, and listen to our intuition. This is not simply a winning formula for times of scarcity; rather, it is a set of ideas that must be added to your personal and business toolkits to ensure success in your endeavours.

First, let's consider the word 'jugaad' as an acronym: J for 'juggle'; U for 'understand'; G for 'guts'; A for 'adapt'; A for 'armour'; and D for 'do-or-die'. By incorporating these terminologies in one's business, one can build a powerful toolkit. This toolkit comprises five easily remembered and practical symbols that will guide you in times of need: the multipurpose hat, the flashlight, the superhero cape, the Swiss Army knife, and the parachute.

The idea of jugaad has been central to my professional and personal life, a collection of values that has guided my family in the business. At its core, jugaad is unconventional innovation that stems from doing more with less – being frugal while solving problems, but not stingy. It calls for innovation that is creative yet unsophisticated, crude yet clever, makeshift yet always up to the mark. Simply put, jugaad is about thinking out of the box so that you can make the most of what you have.

Historically, critics have dismissed and ridiculed Indian family businesses for their use of jugaad in their day-to-day operations. Often, Western and even Indian management gurus have disregarded jugaad as a poor man's makeshift approach to business. In their view, jugaad does not allow for the development of a thriving, modern, and world-class firm. Prominent economist Raghuram Rajan, who previously served as the governor of the Reserve Bank of India was quoted as saying, 'Jugaad is a thoroughly Indian way of coping – it encourages an attitude of shortcuts and evasions, none of which help the quality of final products or sustainable economic growth.'[1] Another criticism thrown at the jugaad approach to business is the idea that it is not scalable. But such experts fail to realize that jugaad can move beyond short-term fixes and towards long-term stability and growth. Mantras of management regularly deployed within family businesses can be polished with a modern twist. A bold and free-spirited mindset can lead to creative, cost-effective, and customizable solutions across many types and sizes of businesses. Simply put, jugaad is the ability to implement a solution against all odds and its beauty lies in its simplicity. It is time to reclaim jugaad as a central principle of business management in India, and even abroad.

Let me give you a personal example of how jugaad can be used to scale. Most businesses usually discover with time that existing systems of information management cannot keep up with their growth and that they need to integrate an enterprise resource planning (ERP) system, such as SAP and Oracle, to help organize the flow of information across all its operations and departments. ERPs, however, are expensive and can have high installation and maintenance costs. Many small businesses baulk at the idea of handing over hundreds of thousands of dollars to integrate one into their daily operations, even if it comes with serious operational benefits.

One such business was ours. MPIL could have benefited from the integration of ERP systems, but investing in one was out of the question, both due to limitations of costs and operational bandwidth. We ultimately opted not to go with an ERP. For us, simply having *a* system in place was more important than the software we used to facilitate that system. We would have been satisfied with a simple paper-driven manual process as well.

We decided to get creative and use an Indian accounting package that cost us ₹367,000 (approximately US$5,000), including user licences and additional taxes, hardware, installations, and maintenance costs. This out-of-the-box choice saved us thousands of dollars while getting us closer to our goal of standardizing processes at our firm. While not as complex as the top-tier ERPs we had considered, the accounting system helped us put transparent systems in place for most of our operations. Using improvised solutions such as manual interventions, paper documentation, and free online tools, we were able to close the data and process loops for records and reports.

We first switched to this makeshift ERP about a decade ago, and the system has since gone through numerous makeovers and upgrades to ensure full optimization. As our business evolved over time (it continues to do so), our solutions needed to evolve along with it. In fact, the accounting system looks completely different today than when we had first commissioned it. We *adapted* as our business grew instead of remaining stagnant. We observed changes in the environment around us and made sure that our tools reflected this change. Our team members continuously collaborated to upgrade and customize the system according to the changing needs of our business. Every transaction, every rule, and every process underwent so many revisions that our evolved makeshift ERP began to perfectly suit our unique needs. Best of all, we were incredibly proud to have achieved this at a low cost, allowing us to invest our funds in the more critical aspects of the business.

Many business owners tend to focus too much on specific methods to achieve a goal at the cost of the goal itself. We lose sight of the destination as we become too worried about the route to get there in the first place. At times we feel the need to reinvent the wheel altogether. But in the end, there might probably be many easier, cheaper, and more efficient ways to get to the same outcome. This is where the jugaad mindset comes into play. It helps businesses overcome the need to follow recommended paths, as well as their attachment to 'best management practices'. Implementing creative solutions does not have to be all about expensive software and technology.

In its early growth stage, a family business can utilize several tools to become more professional and process-oriented. At MPIL, we used simple paper-driven methods. We concocted a hybrid system that was partly manual and partly automated, which our team members could adopt into our daily operations. Dispatch reports and raw material inward summaries came to us by email; at times, the reports were handwritten and scanned, but we did not mind as long as we got the right information at the right time. That is what mattered most when it came to achieving our goals. In recent years, we have even relied heavily on texting and WhatsApp!

Drawing from my experiences at MPIL, I have developed an ultimate survival kit that is particularly relevant for small family-owned businesses which may often not have the resources in hand to accomplish what larger corporations can. This model can be adapted to suit the needs of all types of organizations and explores the strengths inherent to families in business. Instead of reinventing the wheel, all we've got to do is leverage the tools already at our disposal. I will highlight examples from MPIL as well as from other family-managed businesses to show how SMEs have championed change in India, implemented processes, targeted quality and efficiency, increased customer satisfaction, and stayed firmly in business – all through the mindful and unremitting application of this unique toolkit. To begin incorporating the model, all we need are the following:

 Multipurpose Hat: With this tool in hand, individuals can slip into different roles between home and office. An entrepreneur needs to wear multiple hats, especially when navigating a family and a family business together. The hat reminds us to be agile, always on the move and to learn from both our successes and failures.

 Flashlight: It allows us to see clearly and understand the issues at hand. A crucial part of the toolkit, the flashlight illuminates complex matters, encourages deep understanding, teaches us to step back and listen and identifies what is important by helping us focus on the people around us.

 Superhero Cape: The superhero cape allows us to overcome fear and start believing in ourselves, even when we are not feeling brave enough. Fears and anxiety surround us, coming at us from different directions, debilitating our ability to act. When we don our superhero cape, we transform ourselves by leveraging our attitude, thoughts, and network to our advantage.

 Swiss Army Knife: This tool reminds family businesses to leverage their strengths, adjust to situations, and be open to change. The Swiss Army Knife enables us to correct courses quickly. With each new generation entering the family business, change is inevitable, and sometimes external market conditions force us to reinvent ourselves and our business at a far greater pace than we may have anticipated. No bother, as we have the Swiss Army Knife to plan for different outcomes and build a strong armour to remain firm-footed in the face of change.

Parachute: Family-owned businesses regularly confront risk, threat, and anxiety. The last tool in this toolkit, the parachute, reminds us that it is essential to be gutsy at times: to jump in (headfirst) and just 'do.' The emergency parachute embodies the do-or-die spirit, crucial for transformational change.

The Multipurpose Hat: How to Don Multiple Roles

The multipurpose hat, or the safety helmet, serves as a metaphor for the unique roles and responsibilities we often have to undertake. We don different hats to navigate different situations: our thinking hat, our spouse hat, our daughter hat, our manager hat, or our troubleshooter hat. All this while, it is important to protect ourselves, take care of ourselves, and be confident about our actions. Within the first few minutes of arriving at our factory, I would put on this hat, and it's as if everything faded away in the distance. At that moment, my focus would shift to the production floor and the issues at hand. There were days when I would drive back from the factory to the office, arrive late in the evening, switch hats, and deal with the matters there, often entirely different in nature. The hard hat, or shall I say my thinking hat, led me to design my toolkit, so no surprises that it was the first item I added to this toolkit.

The multipurpose hat helps us:

1. Handle multiple responsibilities
2. Keep things moving
3. Learn from every mistake
4. Draw on different disciplines

Handle multiple responsibilities

Notice how entrepreneurs are always jumping between roles, workstreams, and responsibilities? They are their own bosses, but they also need to be versatile and formidable overseers. They must see the big picture but pay attention to the details as well. They must think strategically but also do the grunt work when required.

Entrepreneurs around the world have jugaadu instincts even if they do not explicitly acknowledge them or are even aware of them. It is precisely their talent for juggling multiple roles that propel them to success. Successful entrepreneurs multitask at all levels, expertly judging the time and resources to be invested in various opportunities. They are accustomed to the risk and thrive in uncertainty. Whether they succeed or fail, an entrepreneur always feels their job is never done – the sign of a true entrepreneur. One is almost led to believe that they get a kick out of it!

Leaders may either continue iterating the winning model or move on to bigger projects, no matter how well things are going. And if things aren't going well, they will be driven to find a solution. Family business owners, especially those supported by the active participation of the younger generation, have expanded into multiple businesses fairly rapidly. This is because the younger generation has often come in with greater disruption from technology which, in turn, has speeded up business cycles. Pranav Sayta, a partner at Ernst & Young's family business practice, points out that transitioning from one role to another becomes key for family business owners.[2] Multitasking allows entrepreneurs to do more with limited resources and helps them jump between roles seamlessly. Here, jugaad turns out to be a crucial factor for success because it leads us to aim at the low-hanging fruit first – but with good reason. Facebook's headquarters once featured a sign that said, 'Done is better than perfect.'[3] Perfection can be unattainable at times, but you cannot let its pursuit slow you down.

In 2012, I was delivering a lecture to students of the Family Managed Business programme at SP Jain Institute of Management and Research (SPJIMR), Mumbai. I had invited a young woman named Supriya, who helped design fabrics and patterns for her family business of textile manufacturing, to share her story. She worked out of their corporate office in Mumbai and often felt that unless she started visiting the manufacturing unit near Surat regularly (nearly 200 kilometres), the designer fabrics would not meet her family's expectations. But her family did not allow her to go to the factory on the grounds that the four-hour drive could be unsafe and the rough factory environment would be unsuitable for their daughter. Undeterred, Supriya came up with a way to sell her idea. She asked her parents if they would be okay with her making a weekly trip, accompanied by her driver and a female colleague. She juggled her parents' concerns and the needs of her business and struck a balance that satisfied both parties. Despite their eventual acceptance, her parents still had one non-negotiable demand: that she be back home before 8 p.m.

Supriya now had to wear the multipurpose hat to ensure she used her limited time at the factory to its maximum potential. I greatly enjoyed listening to how she performed this juggling act:

1. *She created a routine*: She decided to go to the factory on a specific day (Tuesday) and stuck to it. It made it easier for her family to get used to the idea.
2. *She found a partner*: Supriya added an additional layer of trust by choosing a female colleague she could work with during her factory visits to assuage her parents' concerns for her safety.

3. *She adapted*: On the days she went to the factory, she dressed in 'modest' attire. This made her parents worry less that their daughter would receive unwanted attention in a remote area.

4. *She set expectations*: She trained her team at the factory to be ready with information and data ahead of her Tuesday visits. She would hit the ground running and accomplish all she needed to get done in just a few hours on the floor (so she could get home before 8 p.m.). For example, she would start with production defects in new designs and seamlessly move to dispatches.

5. *She communicated*: On Tuesdays, while on the way to the factory, she kept in touch with her Mumbai co-workers through open lines of communication even in her absence.

Supriya had skilfully addressed her family's anxieties as well as her responsibilities at work. Her commitment impressed her father. This became the tipping point, after which he unreservedly and unconditionally supported her factory visits, paving the way for her to achieve greater success both at home and in the business.

Keep things moving

One must keep moving to succeed, but how do you decide when and where to move first? To do that, it is important to first prioritize your battles. If you need to take a decision at work, go for it. Making a choice is the hardest part, but remember: if you make a mistake, you can always fix it later.

Success means moving beyond the fear of failure, rather than holding on to your fear of risk. The only thing limiting you is yourself. The key is to remember to move on to the next thing – the next plan, the next iteration, the next option, the next challenge, the next opportunity to deploy jugaad. In family businesses, many of us are wary of how we may be perceived at home for what we do at work. This is also an important source of inspiration for us, to make everyone at home proud. That's why it is important to give family members due credit for their ability to forgive and forget when we do need them to. Self-doubt or your family's perception of you should not deter you from taking decisive action at work.

Learn from every mistake

Wearing protective headgear also means waking up to the realization that one may have been lucky or astute so far, but things may not always continue the same way. Don't take this as a threat; rather, open your eyes to the world. Things change constantly all around us, and we are often limited in our abilities to prevent or stop these changes. When the unexpected Covid-19 pandemic struck in early

2020, most of the world came to a halt. No one in particular, neither the founding generation nor the next gens, could be blamed for the adverse effects of the pandemic on their business.

First- or second-generation family business owners must keep this in mind, especially when a younger generation is being brought into the business, for existing frameworks and systems will be challenged. Things will change. One must be willing to allow the change to play out. The less friction you create, the smoother the path to success will be. As Pramodita Sharma and Allan Cohen articulate in their book *Entrepreneurs in Every Generation: How Successful Family Businesses Develop Their Next Leaders*:[4]

> In generational family firms, the leaders must not only be clear about their own vision for the family enterprise but must also have the courage to acknowledge that the next generation's vision may not be fully synchronized with theirs. It is a delicate art to decide how far to pursue one's own vision and when to 'let go' so as to make room for the next generation's vision to 'take over'.

Though it is often hard (especially as a parent and founder), letting go is a critical part of the business. It is important to let your children make their own mistakes. If you wear the hard hat on their behalf – whether in their personal or professional lives – they will not learn because they are not given the opportunity to do so. Sometimes their screw-ups will be massive, but remember, you still have their backs and will lend a helping hand when truly needed. Help your children calculate and mitigate risks without taking away their sense of ownership. The more trust you place in them and the more independence you grant them, the more they will thrive.

Here, you will have to wear multiple hats as a parent, a silent observer, a hands-on mentor, a supportive friend, and a punching bag all at once. But allow them to put on their hats and experience it for themselves too.

I once needed a subcontractor to ship a steel structure from our factory to a port and then to a container for export. I met with a logistics company. The scope of work sounded straightforward, we discussed the costs involved, and I offered the representative my verbal confirmation. That evening, while driving home with my father, I mentioned that the logistics for the export had been set up. My father asked me about the costs. When I told him the amount, he thought it was high, because the logistics company would first ship the structure from our factory to a stockyard near the port, after which they would load it into a container that would go on a freight ship. Such double handling would cost us more. Instead, my father suggested I look for a company that could bring the container directly to

इबे कीम्मे ना बिगड़्या, इबे तो बेटी बाप के सै।

Ibbe kimme na bigdaya, ibbe toh beti baap ke se

(Nothing has gone wrong yet, because the daughter is still at her father's home)

It's not over until it's over. What if you find out that the man your daughter is engaged to is no good? Isn't it better to find out before the wedding, rather than after? As such, it is important to see things in context and remember that it is never too late to fix a mistake. Made a bad deal, missed a delivery deadline, or forgot to credit a co-worker for their contribution? Pick yourself up, apologize, try harder, and offer some kind of recompense. People are forgiving as long as you are transparent and honest. Do not beat yourself up too much, because nothing is absolute.

our plant and load the material in one shot to go straight onto the ship. In effect, he was asking me to keep things in motion until we had found the best option.

I grew worried. I said I had given the company a verbal confirmation. It would look terrible if I backed out now. He said, 'It's not too late. You haven't issued them a formal work order yet, nor have you released an advance payment.

You cannot make a poor decision just to protect your image. *Ibbe kimme na bigdaya, ibbe toh beti baap ke se.'*

The next morning, I called the company's representative back and apologized for my hasty comments and admitted to them that I was looking for a more reasonably priced solution, one that involved direct loading into a container at our factory itself. Thankfully, the manager of this logistics company was very understanding and appreciated my honesty. We researched some more, now with a better grasp of what we were looking for, and were able to find a price-effective contractor who would bring the container right to our factory door.

Draw on different disciplines

Wearing the multipurpose hat also means you may have to dig in and get your hands dirty at times to challenge your ways of thinking. You will have to find and incorporate elements from different industries, worldviews, experiences, or mindsets to help bring fresh insights. By actively seeking such experiences, you will be able to come up with new ideas that will provide your business with unique and useful benefits. To do so, you will need to draw on learnings from experiences far removed from what you usually do.

Why is this so important to our lives and our businesses? How can one industry benefit from a seemingly different industry or unconnected concept? The key here is to think about the principles that are applied in different fields. While as a civil engineer you may have the tools to read the blueprints of a building, your passion for photography will inform the way you conceptualize and situate the building itself. And because you were on a sports team in college, you know the value of teamwork and team building, while your experience as a teacher might show you how to take initiative, lead the pack, and think for yourself. Do not be afraid to implement varied tools and concepts while trying to break the ice and build bonds at your workplace.

At times, by being too involved in day-to-day operations, we often get absorbed by their familiar rhythms. We develop patterns and routines for problem-solving. What we do not realize is that as much as we shape the business, the business itself often shapes us. Often (and unwittingly) we become like the product or the service we provide – defined, predictable, and perhaps unchanging. Our work informs our worldview and makes us notice things others outside our industry would never consider. Real-estate developers find large empty plots of land interesting, while car enthusiasts may have an eye open for the newest models on the road. But when our frame of reference remains our industry, we may miss the chance to identify new opportunities.

Jugaad requires that we deliberately put an effort behind shaking ourselves out of our daily routine and fixed mindsets. This means finding new interests, taking up new hobbies, discovering new passions, or reading books completely different from the ones we usually do. By stepping outside our comfort zones and spheres of familiarity, we expose ourselves to new ideas that challenge our thinking which will inspire even better ideas and plans.

At MPIL we generate steel scrap, most of which we sell to steel-melting furnaces for very low returns. We had hardly spent any time considering this step of the process since once the scrap was sold, it was out of our purview. We simply tried to optimize our operations to reduce scrap as much as possible and maximize the price we received when we sold it. We would have liked to recycle the scrap, but embarrassingly we never got around to it. There was always something seemingly more urgent to attend to.

As an appreciator of art, I was particularly fascinated by the use of steel in public art structures and always tinkered with the idea of recycling our scrap for this purpose, but had never explored the idea properly. For several years, my interest in public art grew along with an understanding of my business, until one day these two unconnected concepts came together, and I could unite these two distinct worlds and add value in an entirely new way by combining my scrap outflow with my appreciation for the arts.

My friend Elise Foster Vander Elst, founder of Asia Art Projects, is a mover and shaker in the art world. Spending time with her at art galleries, I came across the works of artists around the world who use industrial metals to create innovative and awe-inspiring pieces. Elise once asked me if my factory would be able to provide a light-frame steel structure for one of her artists' installations on the roof of a Mumbai art gallery. It was meant to be a specific text installation that invited multiple interpretations. I immediately said yes, thinking it was nothing more than a simple favour for a dear friend. To get the process started, I asked a junior detailer from our design and engineering department to conceptualize the structure, communicate the plans to the factory, and have two fitters install it for the artist. When the art piece was installed and finally visible to the people of the city, there was widespread excitement in our company. The art's public showcasing turned a personal favour into a special project.

I had not considered our contribution to be substantial; I was simply helping out an old friend. But the pride of my employees was contagious and made me realize that all of us were hungry for opportunities that let us do more with the tools, resources, and skills we already possessed. The British creator of the piece, Emma Gamble, gifted me a framed photo of the installation – a photo that hangs in my office to this day. Not only is her art inspiring in itself, but it is also a constant reminder that the more divergent, contrasting, and new elements I bring into my work, the more my business will benefit. Here is a picture of the installation on the roof of the Studio-X Mumbai gallery in Colaba, which reads 'THIS MESSAGE IS A SIGN FROM ABOVE'.

With the success of this project and insights from Elise, I decided to mix these two worlds to see what more I could create. I recruited my brother's friend and renowned Spanish-American artist Armando Miguelez to visit our factory and see if he would be inspired by our scrap steel to create his next art project. Armando's work explores the ways in which the physical world is organized, with a specific focus on cartography and systems of world measurement. His work contemplates issues of personal narrative, displacement, cultural contrasts, and architecture. His artistic inspiration was a perfect match for what our plant had to offer. Armando presented Elise and me with a concept note for a work titled *Retribution*, which was essentially a large-scale steel artwork he planned to create in our very factory with recyclable steel. *Retribution* was to be a six-metre-tall steel piece shaped like a balance scale, which typically symbolizes justice, equality, or fairness. Once the structure was complete, large blocks of ice were to be placed on both sides of the scale representing the fleeting nature of an element in transition – the ephemeral nature of what is perceived as permanent.

From our head office to our plant, everyone was excited to get on board with the project. It was like any other project we had executed, with the team working together to design the piece, source the materials, have the engineers cut and weld steel plates, and so on. However, it had the added excitement of producing something creative and new, which inspired everyone to work even harder. Armando's easygoing charm and extroverted personality helped too. Not only was he able to work with the team, but was also able to win them over as friends by the end of the project.

Once finished, Armando's project had all of us floored. My family in particular loved the piece and what it stood for. He had used a basic yet powerful symbol, something everyone could relate to and understand. It also allowed observers and visitors to engage with the installation and come to their own interpretations. Moreover, within four months of the creation of *Retribution*, all the scrap pieces from our plant had been transformed into public art. As a company, we enjoyed numerous benefits. We were applauded in art circles as a 'cool' steel firm, which helped us expand our network, gain entry into circles previously unknown to us, and got us newfound recognition as a firm.

We also received plenty of free press and media attention. Magazines such as *Marie Claire*, *Atelier*, and *Verve* wrote articles about our association with the art piece. Further, when the US Consul General in Mumbai, Peter Haas, inaugurated the art piece at our plant, it led to further positive media coverage. We were also able to maximize the value of the recyclable steel stored at our plant by exploring an entirely new avenue of value-added services. We had transformed our steel into a permanent piece of art, installed in our factory's front lawn for all to enjoy as a public good. This experience of using our steel as an element for public art got us excited and we were now ready for more art projects in the future.

At the end of the day, as an organization, we learned what monumental art pieces can say about the social realities around us. The opportunity to engage with the arts through Armando and Elise was a valuable learning experience, one that deepened our understanding of the world beyond industrial steel construction. *Retribution* led to the formation of MPIL & The Arts, an initiative to explore ways to invest in human capital and public art. We had essentially applied the principles of jugaad to transcend cultures, industries, and mindsets.

Here are a few pictures showing our progress from start to finish:

Parth Jindal, third-generation leader of the JSW Group, has been a pioneer in channelling his corporate resources towards supporting Indian sports and developing Indian athletes. Leveraging the infrastructure at their Vijayanagar plant, Parth helped set up the Inspire Institute of Sport, as India's first privately funded performance training centre to train athletes in different sports. For his encouragement towards sports and corporate social responsibility initiatives to launch sustainable athlete-centric initiatives, Parth won the national Khel Protsahan Puruskar in 2019.

When each team or family member tries to solve internal problems using skills they have developed through their other interests, it can lead to a different and fruitful conversation for the business. Fresh (and balanced) ideas help all stakeholders find common ground. In our family business, for instance, we often combine our interests with our professional work. Our social interactions with friends inform our HR policies and recruitment; our travels inform our business development; our family culture informs the support network we create for women at MPIL; and so on. Applying jugaad is to regularly compare and contrast concepts, worldviews, and ideas by trying out different lenses to look at life. Each lens will bring a new perspective about the same situation while stimulating our minds to come up with innovative solutions we may not have discovered yet.

The Flashlight: How to See Clearly

Explorers and adventurers consider the flashlight to be an integral part of their journey. We need it to cut through the darkness, or metaphorically cut through the noise and clutter, to be able to see and think clearly. It helps us shine a light on what's at the heart of an issue and illuminates the perspectives of others. The light inspires humility, allowing us to give in to others, listen and pay attention, and value their input. This powerful tool serves many useful purposes and has thus earned its place in this toolkit.

The flashlight reminds us to:
1. Take a deep dive
2. Talk less, listen more
3. Ask the right questions
4. Believe in *Ubuntu*

Take a deep dive

The flashlight helps us see clearly by cutting through the darkness and helping us find what we are looking for. This clarity comes with a deep understanding of the situation in front of us. My **U-Model** is based on the idea that a deep

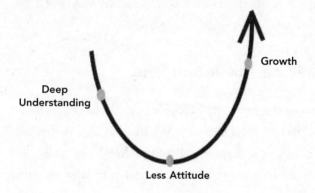

knowledge of your field and an un-presuming attitude towards your employees can provide a springboard for growth.

Deep Understanding: The initial downward arc of the U-Model represents the need for a deep dive to understand the essential details of your field. You can build this knowledge in several ways. The first thing to do is to discuss issues with pertinent stakeholders. Some of the most insightful information comes about through qualitative discussions with the relevant parties. An open conversation allows people to explain their viewpoints in depth, providing clarity that would otherwise be missing. One needs to move beyond one's immediate circle, and speak to competitors, subordinates, suppliers, and unrelated industry professionals to broaden their vision.

The second way to get a deeper understanding is through industry conferences and learning material such as industry-specific magazines. Though a passive way of learning, such methods hold tremendous value. These mediums tend to feature new trends and shine the spotlight on complex industry-specific concepts you may not have understood or been unaware of previously.

And finally, one must learn new skills, no matter what stage in life or business one currently is in. As technology becomes increasingly accessible, democratized, and disruptive, those who fail to stay on the learning curve will soon find themselves falling behind. Upskilling (continuous learning, especially in newer fields) is now integral to staying relevant in a professional capacity.

Consider someone like Akshay Modi, who is today the managing director of his family's firm, Modi Naturals. Modi originally faced many difficulties while trying to integrate himself into the company after returning from abroad. Recognizing that he could not easily figure out where to place himself, he decided to join a research firm, which inspired in him new ideas for Modi Naturals. He dove deep into businesses and markets and was well-equipped to add value once he re-joined the family business. In fact, he was so successful in his quest to gain a 'deeper understanding' that he rolled out new products, rebranded and renamed the company, targeted new consumers, and launched R&D efforts – all based on his research, knowledge, insights, and learnings – which helped grow the firm into a market leader.[4] This is the sort of deep dive that marks the beginning of a successful business.

गुरू गुड़ रह गया, चेला चीनी बन गया

Guru gud reh gaya, chela chini ban gaya

(The student has become the master)

Jaggery and sugar are both sweeteners derived from sugarcane. Jaggery is an unrefined product extracted from sugarcane juice by simply boiling it. Sugar, on the other hand, is created by refining the syrup with charcoal which leaves behind sugar as a crystalline residue. Even though jaggery has been used for much longer as a sweetener, the refinement process leaves sugar with a better taste and look. Today, sugar has surpassed jaggery in both sales and popularity. The same parallel can be drawn with leaps that next gens take by building on the previous generations' work. With fresh energy, knowledge of new technology, and markets, the next gen turns the *gud* (jaggery) – containing potent learnings gained with experience – humbly passed on by the older generation into *chini* (sugar). An apt example can be found in Himanshu Gupta, a third-generation entrepreneur under whose leadership S. Chand Publishing has undergone a major digital transformation. Himanshu has built upon the traditional textbook publishing business set up by his grandfather, Shyam Lal Gupta, in 1939.

Less attitude: The next turn in the U-Model highlights the need for humility. A haughty demeanour throws up walls around that hinder your understanding and reduce your standing in the minds of the people around you. For instance, consider the importance of keeping various avenues of discussion open. You will not be able to achieve your goals if you went into such conversations with a fixed mindset, preconceived notions, or an attitude of self-importance. Good leadership requires the ability to put yourself in the shoes of your customers and employees, which requires both empathy and humility. If you throw away your pride, you may end up with a clearer view of how things work. The concept of jugaad centres around what is possible when we stop fixating on top-down R&D efforts and instead allow for organic, bottom-up innovation. Instead of dismissing these ideas as a poor man's thought process thinking, open yourself to grassroots solutions created and devised in consultation with customers, colleagues, peers, or even family. You may end up with something far simpler and better targeted towards the needs of your organization and your customer.

Growth: Once equipped with a deep understanding and a humble attitude, one can achieve growth that spans several dimensions beyond pure financial gain.
- **Profitable growth:** Profit is the first measure most people think of when they hear 'growth' and 'business' in the

same sentence. The twin factors – deep understanding and low attitude – can help cut costs and increase revenue. For instance, an honest conversation with your stakeholders will allow you to understand their needs better. If you convert these insights into actions, you can offer them products and services that suit them better, thereby increasing your sales.

- **Employee growth**: Employee growth and development can take a variety of forms. You can offer employees on-the-job training, webinars, or even sponsor external training for them. This would also allow them to take up more responsibilities and develop the skills necessary for their role in the company.

- **Growth in the community:** A family business must always consider the market in which it operates. It may be concerned with increasing its goodwill and reputation in a locality, as it is not only the brand but the family name that comes under scrutiny. It therefore becomes important to consider your current portfolio of relationships, especially with local businesses. Are you a good vendor for your customers? Are you a respectful client for your suppliers? There's also reputational growth within your industry to consider. For instance, are you willing to serve as a knowledge partner to help others grow? Have you made efforts to build and sustain a local network of peers? Moreover, what about individuals in your community? Are you an empathetic employer who allows workers to spend time with their families? Do you monitor the noise pollution level at your factories or the traffic issues caused by your trucks? Try to build a 360-degree view of your firm to develop and grow in your community instead of being a solitary player.

- **Sustainable growth:** Environmental considerations are often perceived as a hindrance to growth. But clients across industries are becoming increasingly concerned about the environmental impact of their activities. Developing a sustainability strategy for your company helps position it as a forward-looking partner. Taking actionable steps to implement the strategy will show your firm's commitment and trustworthiness – not just to the environment, but to its other responsibilities as well. An investment today in greener technologies, systems, and initiatives, will end up benefiting you tremendously a few years down the line.

Talk less, listen more

Our business involves selling steel building components to contractors, who then install these structures at construction sites across India. We wanted to increase our sales via the contractor supply chain by providing additional resources to support our contractors but were not sure how we could do so. We held internal discussions about our sales strategy and would incorporate client feedback at times, but never in a structured or organized way. One day, fortuitously, we ended up having a probing conversation with a contractor who had come into our office. He told us that while he understood what his end client needed, he did not have the resources to put together a proper technical presentation, with 3-D images and a datasheet for the client. The datasheet needed to include a Bill of Quantities (BoQ), which he could not produce. The BoQ would have given the end client an exact list of all the steel parts he would have needed for a particular project.

I realized our company's detailing and engineering division could be looped in to generate the BoQ for our contractors. With this knowledge in hand, we launched a system through which every subcontractor buying our steel would get free technical data service. Not only has this brought about growth in our sales over the last few years, but also instilled the contractors with confidence in the services we provide. They saw the value we brought to their business as well as our efforts to strengthen our relationship with them. We could have launched a complex research survey that would have brought the same result, but we managed to come up with a successful sales strategy by interacting with and understanding our contractors.

Listening brings one great value. If you are ready to listen, you can pick up critical information whenever you meet someone – whether an employee, a vendor, a client, an investor, and especially a competitor. Show genuine interest in their personal and professional lives, ask them questions, understand their passion, and see if there is an opportunity for you to follow up or even work with them. Building a relationship is difficult and should not just be transactional.

Alok Khetan is the second-generation family business leader of the international Multibis Group, a manufacturing and distribution company with a large presence in Nigeria, India, and the UAE, among other countries. Alok's father, who founded the group, was one of the first Indian businessmen to venture into West Africa for business prospects almost forty-two years ago. When Alok joined the business, he spent a significant amount of time, shadowing his father, getting to know key stakeholders over one-on-one meetings, asking questions and simply observing. He worked on the ground in Nigeria for the first couple of years, before moving to the Singapore office and eventually to Dubai to set up the UAE office. Alok's advice to the next generation joining their family business is to be patient, extremely patient, and to learn and soak in as much detail and nuance as they can.

Alok has been able to introduce many systems and processes into his business to improve employee accountability and performance. He has been able to make information accessible and available on a real-time basis. He was able to achieve this by closely watching each aspect of his business and through numerous conversations with his stakeholders to figure out where the roadblocks are. Alok said to me, 'The younger generation is impatient. They come in, and they immediately want to make changes. They want to scrap this, scrap that.' However, Alok believes, only after you delve deeper and listen will you realize that there is a reason why things have worked in a certain way and you cannot bring about meaningful change without that background knowledge.

Ask the right questions

What are the other ways to acquire more knowledge? The obvious answer is by asking as many questions as possible, but at the same time, one must ask the *right* questions. Genuine understanding comes from throwing yourself into your field as deeply as possible. But knowledge can also come from putting yourself in uncomfortable situations, asking people complex questions, and trying to get answers no matter the obstacles. The responses will lead you to new opportunities. Push yourself into unknown territory. Displace yourself both physically and mentally to understand how the world operates, how and why things matter, and why people do what they do. The questions may unnerve you, but they will force you to question your assumptions about the world and experience the humbling effect of the talent and expertise that surround you.

When my brother and I were young, we would regularly turn to our father with questions: about our school, about why things were how they were, about literally anything under the sun. He would answer them to the best of his ability or eventually find us a suitable answer. He was onto something crucial – he wanted to develop a sense of curiosity in his children, curiosity that would serve us well when we become adults. As he says, 'Answers are easy to find. The harder thing is to frame the right question.'

Isha Ambani, next-gen business leader of Reliance Industries, sowed the seeds of India's largest digital services platform Jio. She was frustrated by the internet speed in her house and questioned why India could not have faster internet and more widespread access, just like some countries in the West. Out of such questions was born Reliance's venture into providing high-speed internet, telephony, television, video streaming, and many more digital services on a massive scale in India.

Believe in Ubuntu or humanness

The South African Bantu word 'ubuntu' has a beautiful translation: 'I am, because you are.' It refers to the universal bond that connects all of humanity. Ubuntu is central to our survival kit; it is one of the key aspects that distinguishes family businesses from their corporate counterparts. The flashlight metaphor shines a light on the humanity of family businesses which places people at their centre. Ubuntu reminds us that an inclusive and grassroots-oriented approach can nurture employees and enable customer-led creativity. It challenges elitism and hierarchy and opens up decision-making to communal and participatory improvisation. Speaking from personal experience, Tina Fey, well-known American comedian and actress, talks about the importance of being a 'considerate co-worker.'[5] Her advice is to be kind, to help colleagues in small meaningful ways at work, and to cover for them when they need to run an errand without being a tattletale about it.

John Elkington's 'Triple Bottom Line' framework suggests that a firm's performance should be measured in three dimensions.[6] In addition to profits, a firm must be measured by its people and its impact on the planet. These three P's provide a new way of looking at a business: they examine the business's effect on the world and its employees. These concepts are inalienable to family businesses and ubuntu, as it is only through a genuine connection with the community that one can create useful business solutions.

In India, family businesses have historically been able to integrate social responsibility with sustainable development goals. Mr Krishnaraj Vanarayar B. K., founder of the Nallamuthu Gounder Mahalingam

College in Coimbatore, an institution leading triple bottom-line initiatives, points out that family businesses in Coimbatore, inspired by the teachings of Mahatma Gandhi, have been contributing to social causes, even before a formal national CSR policy had mandated it by law.[7] Sajjan Jindal, managing director of the JSW Group, shares an anecdote about how his father Shri O. P. Jindal looked for ways to create value for society. Once a team from Germany came to meet the senior Jindal for potential collaborations. During their discussions, Sajjan Jindal recalls, the Germans asked his father why he was looking to set up a small plant, whereas the trend in the rest of the world was to opt for bigger plants. To this, he had replied, 'Our economy is different from yours. We have limitations when it comes to capital. More than that, I have a social responsibility to create more jobs.'[8]

In 2010, I set up the MPIL Circle of Trust, which was an initiative to capture our best practices and highlight the strengths of MPIL as an ideal employer. Now a sub-group within our organization, it recognizes the efforts of long-term employees and builds a support network for them to foster growth opportunities within the company. The criteria for selection into the trust embodies the fundamental qualities we value in our team members, which include efficiency, curiosity, growth, loyalty, and ingenuity. Employees who have completed three years within the organization can apply to be a member. Two members of the management team interview the shortlisted candidates, and if they pass this final round, we welcome them into that year's batch, thus continually growing the group. Being a member of the trust has become a milestone that brings out the best in our employees. Most importantly, it rewards those who have shown exemplary performance and dedication towards the organization. Such recognition helps solidify our community at MPIL and forge stronger bonds across our workforce.

The idea for the Circle of Trust took root when I was conducting recruitment interviews for various departments. Every weekend, I would interact with candidates of different ages, skill sets, and backgrounds, which gave me a deep understanding of what candidates looked for in a job. Their hunger for growth and their excitement to learn impressed me. Their sense of loyalty was tied to the ability to exercise independence within the organization. This, in turn, meant that for us to retain and develop human talent, we had to offer something more than monetary compensation – a playground to run around, a laboratory where they could experiment, and a safety net to support them along the way. If we could launch such a programme, our competitors would not have an edge over us or be able to poach our team members easily.

When I launched the initiative in 2010, the response was overwhelming. I formulated a simple open-ended questionnaire and circulated it among employees who had been with the organization for over three years. A few of the questions were:

- What would you like to do differently this year?
- Would you like more or less responsibility?
- Would you like to learn about some other aspect of this industry?
- Would you like to change departments?
- How can we help you grow at MPIL?

The responses we received demonstrated that our employees were willing to open up about their career goals and aspirations. Their answers were thoughtful and articulated their vision for themselves within our organization. As management representatives, we were energized by their vigour and ambition. Some employees wanted a wider job profile, while others wanted a change of location. Still others felt they were ready for increased responsibilities.

The questionnaire was the beginning of a new dialogue between the employees and the management, which helped us curate career growth plans tailored for the unique needs of each employee. In addition to being a badge of honour, members of the trust enjoy several privileges and monetary benefits. For example, they have the flexibility to plan their leaves as per their needs, the company subsidizes their children's education fees, they can take a free trip home during their holidays, among other perks. Every year we make sure to review and modify the list of benefits, taking into consideration employee feedback.

The flashlight helps you shine a light on what matters the most in a family business: people. It helps you remember to focus on people, listen to them, be patient with them, and to invest in them. This is made possible by a deep-rooted family value system that privileges humanity over everything.

The Superhero Cape: How to Work Past Fear

Superheroes are synonymous with courage and action. They are the ultimate saviours who selflessly jump in to help others. Each of them comes with unique powers and some transform from a common individual into a superhero as they put on their cape. This cape then becomes a metaphor for the courage to act, the ability to do the unthinkable, to lead, and to set an example for others. Most of the next-gen family business members I spoke to talked about being afraid, nervous, or hesitant. This led me to include the cape in the kit, because sometimes, we need to pull ourselves out of the circles of doubt and elevate ourselves to a higher level, in order to act fearlessly. The superhero cape may be the most powerful tool in this survival kit because it counters the most common fears all of us face.

The superhero cape reminds us to:

1. Push past our fears
2. Have the courage to act

Push past our fears

In an ever-changing and interconnected world, businesses must adapt quickly to thrive and survive. Risks and threats – such as competitors, new regulations, economic downturns, and environmental crises – mean that business leaders need to be prepared for whatever the world throws at them. Leaders who welcome risk, adversity, and challenges with courage and open arms are often rewarded. These leaders derive energy from within and by interacting with others. They are intrinsically motivated individuals whose true passion shines through their work. They may be quiet, or they may be loud, but each one of them has the guts to follow their ambitions.

Take a minute to think about some of the most influential and impactful business leaders you know. For me, it is Mr Sajjan Jindal, India's man of steel, whose resolve and 'fire in the belly' has steered him away from the stress of being a businessman. Speaking to the *Economic Times* in 2013, Mr Jindal said, 'I have faced a number of crises in my career. But every time I am hit with a crisis, I always tell my staff that there's an opportunity in it. So, rather than get[ting] worried or bogged down by the crisis, start looking for the opportunity."[9]

The superhero cape in our toolkit reminds us to find our courage. Essentially, one must possess the emotional courage to pursue ideas and see them through to the very end. In other words, one must channel a sense of focus and the ability to jump in headfirst without always waiting for the 'right time' or the 'right opportunity'. One must have the guts to think big, think out of the box, and think as if absolutely nothing is impossible. A leader must possess the courage to face people and situations boldly and see to it that an idea is followed through all the way from its conception to its execution.

We all know these kinds of people; there are many examples all around us. The guy who started his own multimillion-dollar business out of his garage. The woman who is running five companies simultaneously. Your colleague who seems to know every single person at a networking event. Your peer who ran with a crazy startup idea, even when others said the business would not make it, and is now a successful entrepreneur. These are the people you call when you need something done, when the rubber hits the road or when times get tough. Take, for example, the dynamic Akshay Narvekar, founder of Bombay Shirt Company, India's first online custom-made, wholly personalized shirt brand. While many may look at the large Indian apparel and retail industry and be wary of entering such a competitive space, Akshay was bold and astute to see an opportunity for disruption. His concepts stores, where carefully crafted shirts are tailor-made, have grown to multiple outlets within India and in Dubai and New York.[10]

Our doubts and self-imposed limitations are often the main hindrances to our success. We become our loudest critics, we think everyone is waiting for us to slip up. Irrational, rational, or unreal, such fear is truly paralyzing. Instead of listening to our gut instincts and channelling our energies towards our goals, we worry about the 'what ifs': What if my idea is stupid? What if no one likes it? What if I cannot get this thing off the ground? What if I lose money? What if I make a mistake? What if no one believes in me? Funnily enough, we put so much weight into the future when it has not even happened yet.

Divert your energies from worrying about things you have not yet encountered towards what is in your control at the moment, and you will find yourself empowered to take charge of the situation.

Have the courage to act

Ideas pop up in our heads almost on a daily basis. Some may be ingenious solutions to world problems, others just a simple fix to an everyday obstacle. But most ideas are never translated to reality. Think about the ideas you have had throughout your life. How many of them have materialized? Maybe the idea had not been fully thought out. Maybe you the time to pursue it or did not have the tools or resources to explore further. Or maybe you did not think it was a good idea.

An entrepreneur with a plan is simply someone who has the courage to allow his idea to go beyond the mind. Such entrepreneurs do not focus on the what-ifs of an idea; they just *do*. Successful business leaders trust their instinct. Drawing from years of experiences, learnings, networks, and contacts, they develop an intangible but essential intuition that guides them forward.

Letting go of fear to move ahead with an idea is only the first step. How does one bring in the momentum to turn an idea into reality? Sure, your friends, family, peers, colleagues, or shareholders may buy your idea, but without a clear sense of mission shaped by your own instincts, your idea will never reach its full potential. As a business owner or entrepreneur, it is critical to reflect on the 'why' behind an idea: why do you want to implement it? You have to understand the driving force behind your idea first. This will not only help you tailor your plans, but also have the secondary effect of allowing you to exude a contagious level of confidence and enthusiasm. In short, reflecting on what motivates you will give you confidence, which in turn will bring a sense of gusto to your mission.

In their book, *Heart, Smarts, Guts, and Luck: What It Takes to Be an Entrepreneur and Build a Great Business*, entrepreneurs Anthony Tjan, Richard Harrington, and Tsun-Yan Hsieh bring decades of their experiences from the world of venture capital, advising, and management to develop an aptitude tool. This tool draws on hundreds of interactions with business leaders globally. They identify four key qualities – hearts, smarts, guts, and luck (HSGL) – typically found in successful leaders and entrepreneurs in varying degrees or combinations. Let us break down these four attributes further:

- **Heart-dominant:** These leaders are driven by purpose and passion, sacrifice for the greater good, and have a nuanced approach. Heart-dominant individuals are 'the artists of the business world' and may be described as founders or visionaries. They are often found running small and medium-sized enterprises.

- **Smarts-dominant:** These leaders are driven by facts and logic, accountability, and strategy. Smarts-dominant individuals make decisions rationally and analytically. They consider patterns, past experiences, and other viewpoints and opinions before taking a decision. They innovate and create in a methodical manner.

- **Guts-dominant:** These leaders are driven by risk and change and are not held back by fear. They are known for taking bold steps. When things get tough, they are the ones people turn to for leadership, guidance, and direction. They persevere, manage risk, and multitask well.

- **Luck-dominant:** These leaders are driven by intellectual curiosity, optimism, and humility, built on a foundation of preparedness. Luck-dominant individuals are characterized by their 'lucky attitude' and a 'lucky network'. They believe in possibility and serendipity.

Most may think that a business plan is fundamental to the establishment of any business. Most see it as the first step. However, the authors argue that a business plan may in fact be a disadvantage, *especially* in the early stages, because it may cause leaders to overthink, focus on irrelevant details, and miss the big picture. The authors found that nearly 70 percent of successful founders did not start with a business plan. So instead of starting with a plan, the authors recommend starting the business first – jump out of that parachute; then you can figure out how to open it. This is especially true for heart-dominant individuals who may be more likely to act out of passion and impulse. Take that first step, see what works; if it doesn't work out, go back to the drawing board, keep iterating and testing until you get it right.

Often we do not realize that our strengths can be our weaknesses, and vice versa. Identifying your strengths as a leader is key to exploiting them; however, it is equally important to understand how these strengths can manifest as weaknesses so that you can mitigate the negative effects. For instance, if you are too detail-oriented, make sure you have someone on your team who will remind you to zoom out. If you start too fast, have a partner good at setting the stage and doing background research. If you are prone to making hasty decisions, institute idea-sharing meetings to solicit your employees' opinions.

In family businesses, we find that often the founding or older generations are more likely to be guts-dominant or luck-dominant, whereas next gens are prone to smarts-dominant behaviour. In 2015, as a Global Shaper for the World Economic Forum, I moderated a family business talk at which my fellow Shaper, Alisha Chona Shah, third-generation leader of the famous Mumbai restaurant Cream Centre, shared her experience with us. Alisha's grandfather Ramesh Chona set up Cream Centre in 1952; it is situated right on the Queen's Necklace. The restaurant served a wide variety of vegetarian dishes because her grandfather realized only after acquiring the space for the restaurant that it was located in a Jains-only building. The restaurant became immensely popular among vegetarian communities. Together with her father, Sanjeev Chona, Alisha has transformed the restaurant and its menu with a modern interior and style, all the while retaining the original favourites. Alisha is business savvy and understood the kind of experience a modern-day consumer desires. And when her father wasn't sure about making Cream Centre a pan-India chain, she donned her superhero cape and led the initiative with her guts and smarts to expand to twelve cities and then onto international cities like Dubai.[11]

In *StrengthsFinder 2.0.*, renowned author and consultant Tom Rath, helps us understand our professional selves so that we can take advantage of our best qualities and assets. Most of us may not be aware of our natural talents and are thus not able to activate them in our professional lives. The idea is to uncover and identify natural talents to exploit them for our benefit. As per *StrengthsFinder 2.0*, talent is associated with natural patterns of thoughts and behaviour; paired with the right role, they help achieve greater self-awareness and improved performance. The book offers readers a chance to assess their top five strengths from an array of qualities ranging from achiever to maximizer to includer. Thereon, Rath offers hundreds of strategies to apply those strengths towards success across thirty-four different themes through vignettes, advice, and 'ideas for action'. As he says, 'You cannot be anything you want to be – but you can be a lot more of who you already are.'[12] This framework can be used to better identify the core strengths of each family member in the business, to appreciate their roles and to assign them responsibilities that leverage their pre-existing abilities.

For a family coming together to make business decisions, the superhero cape reminds us to use resources like the StrengthsFinder thinking to achieve fruitful dialogue. For instance, in our family, our mother's strength is 'harmony' and can be classified as the 'relator', always trying to make sure everyone is at ease and in agreement. My brother, the 'analyzer', enjoys considering different points of views. I realized that I was inclined to be 'restorative', quick to prescribe solutions, and needed to give my family members space to arrive at their own choices. My father, who feels tremendous 'responsibility' felt he had to do every single thing himself. After taking the test and discovering a new vocabulary to discuss our behaviour, we developed a deeper understanding of our individual perspectives and more patience to deal with one another.

The idea behind the superhero cape is that it is not necessary to reinvent the wheel every time. Focus on your existing strengths and use them to remind yourself there is no reason to fear the unknown. Use the experience and the past that have led you to where you are. Use your fears as fuel. If you can do that, you will discover the confidence that will give you the momentum, energy, and passion you need to drive your idea home.

काम करने के सौ तरीक़े हैं और काम ना करने के भी सौ तरीक़े हैं।

Kaam karne ke sau tareeke hain, aur kaam na karne ke bhi sau tareeke hain

(There are a hundred ways to do something, and just as many ways to not do something)

Humans are wired to immediately focus on the negatives to reduce risk. It is a precautionary trait ingrained into our DNA. However, by only focusing on the negatives, we miss out on the positives that a decision may bring. Try to flip the script and first look at the positive aspects. Doing so will bring a different energy and help you look at a problem from a different angle.

My father is a guts-dominant business leader: unafraid, bold, clear, and confident. He can come up with an action plan and see it through without a problem. He uses this quote whenever someone tries to list out the negative outcomes of a proposed plan. Instead, his approach is to start with the affirmative, and list the ways by which a result *can be* achieved. For sure, the solutions for potential challenges need to be thought through too. But you must give precedence to the ways you can actually realize your plan. By doing so, you will find that failure is only in your head most of the time. If we rewire ourselves to think positively, we can get all the more closer to success.

The Swiss Army Knife: How to Adapt to Change

A Swiss Army knife is a collection of tools neatly packaged to fit in one's pocket, making it versatile and easy to carry around. It may have a blade, a screwdriver, a can opener, a nail file, a pair of scissors or combinations of other small tools. The Swiss Army knife has become a popular cultural metaphor for usefulness and adaptability; its multipurpose nature inspires versatility. How fortunate it is to have this tool in our own family business survival kit, allowing us to hone our skills, improve our adaptivity, and enable us to change our course as required. It reminds us to tweak here and there to fine-tune our work with our nail file or cut ties with our scissors or start over with a can opener. The tools of the Swiss Army knife are at play all the time, every single day, and many of us use them without realizing it. My husband gifted me a Swiss Army knife when we were dating, and I had thought of it as a rather curious present at the time. But once I attached it to my key chain, I began using it all the time. I would open envelopes and packages with the blade, cut strings and tape with scissors. I did not realize how much I needed it till I had one. I also felt like a total badass pulling it out because it always elicited a reaction from those around me. And that's why I have my actual and metaphorical Swiss Army knife with me at all times.

The Swiss Army knife helps us:
1. Adapt to different situations
2. Devise the right armour
3. Course-correct as required

Adapt to different situations

Family businesses often require individuals to be adaptable to change, given the diverse roles they are expected to play. Having family members on board is a necessary part of decision-making, but more importantly, in ensuring long-term success. But getting people with different agendas, interests, and backgrounds to agree with one another is often quite difficult, and requires individuals to adapt to the situation.

In many family businesses, the founder may simply lay down the law and take a unilateral decision that other family members are expected to follow. A more adaptive attitude from the younger generations can help steer the older generation away from their stubborn stances. They have to be adept at communicating and careful about their words, tone, and even gestures. They must choose strategies that will resonate with those they are trying to win over. Sometimes, all they have to do is convey the same message in different ways for different audiences. For example, my brother and I try to plant the seeds of a new idea in our father's mind in such a way that as we continue to discuss the idea, he begins to believe it was his idea all along.

So how does one use adaptability to get what one wants? One way is to give credit to the person whose approval you seek. Empathize with them by placing yourself in their shoes and try to understand the interests and incentives that motivate them. In turn, you can tap into their empathy by telling them about the challenges you face, asking for advice, or seeking their blessings for a new idea or venture. Assure them you will not move forward without their support. Share your passion and show them why you are excited and offer to share this excitement with them. Publicly acknowledge their support. Accept their feedback (whether positive or negative) with a positive attitude and try to incorporate it wherever possible. At the same time, be honest about the risks. The engagement has to be a genuine dialogue. Always remember that having family members on your side can be advantageous for you.

Tina Fey, in her book *Bossypants*, talks about a useful technique, drawing from her background in improv comedy.[13] She describes the rules of improvisation which can be applied to the context of working with family members. The first rule is to agree, to say yes. When improvising, you are required to agree with whatever your co-worker has suggested. While this is not always possible, it is an important reminder to respect your family member's opinion and address it with an open mind. Be open to being swayed by where a yes may take you, encourages

Tina. The second rule of improvisation is to take the 'yes' a little further to a 'yes, and'. This means that you not only agree with your co-worker but also contribute something meaningful. This facilitates the flow of thoughts and ideas. The third rule of improvisation is to offer solutions, to make statements, not just badger them with a string of questions or pessimism. I find these simple rules remarkably helpful. They help us introspect our personal attitude towards those we work with.

Devise the right armour

The Swiss Army knife helps you create an adequate armour, to work out a backup plan, particularly in the context of creating additional support for your actions. This will require you to rely on your networks and tap into all your resources. Finally, it means building a flexible roadmap with the understanding that things are bound to change so that when they do, you are ready to adjust.

If you have an innovative idea, it is critical that you prepare several versions of the same concept. Identify how your idea can evolve, particularly the components that are more susceptible to external influence. Such flexibility will allow you to incorporate change and feedback more easily. You might have a vision, but you should be aware of the chinks in your armour, the different ways in which you may slip up or fail.

It is not enough to simply identify those chinks, just as it is not enough to identify a problem without thinking of a solution. After identifying possible avenues of challenges, prepare a roadmap that allows you to regroup and respond in the right manner. This ensures your plan does not die if worst comes to worst. If the first iteration is not entirely successful, that is alright. Maintain a jugaadu attitude; it makes you ingenious, creative, agile, and optimistic, and therefore, well prepared to change course and try something new. If your armour is built ahead of time, you will be ready to face whatever comes your way.

One of the examples of being ready with an 'adequate armour' comes from the matrimonial site Bharat Matrimony. The company was doing exceptionally well in the online space, but it wanted to expand its offline presence as well. They realized there were few 'live' opportunities for young singles interested in marriage to meet up and decided to become a first mover in a space that had not yet been explored. So, it set up physical booths in shopping malls, where young people and their parents could come, sign up, and register their profile in person for the company to find them a match.

Unfortunately, the offline venture failed to take off. When I spoke to the founder of Bharat Matrimony, Murugavel Janakiramen, at a talk at the Tata Institute of Social Sciences in Mumbai, he said he had come to realize that the main issue with the offline model was a lack of anonymity. Although young singles put up their profiles with names, pictures, age, and other personal information online, they were uncomfortable with openly seeking out and approaching a matrimonial booth at a public venue. However, he did not let the hiccup deter him. He was sufficiently prepared to address his customers' concerns and tweaked the model to set up a private consulting service. He solved the problem with a simple and elegant solution. Meetings could now be set up at a customer's home, office, or venue of choice, allowing parents and singles to get to know the other family in a more private setting. This service was well received and hugely successful. Muruga was willing to go back to square one, reconsider his customers' needs, and relaunch a slightly tweaked version of the original plan.

Having the right armour to back you up prepares you for possible strategy fails. Failure may be a part of life, but that does not mean you have to give up altogether. If, over the course of your career, you weld an impenetrable armour that protects you in the face of adversity, you will find it easier to go right back into the fray and try till you succeed. After all, if you fail at something, you have the best chance of success next time around, simply because you are not starting from ground zero. By learning from your mistakes, you will be able to build a strong armour to revisit your ideas without losing hope, passion, or dedication.

Course-correct as required

Like the Swiss Army knife that can swiftly assemble, dissemble, and repair, we have to be ready to do the same for our businesses too. The basis of this idea comes from Reid Hoffman's *The Start-up of You: Adapt to the Future, Invest in Yourself, and Transform Your Career*, in which Hoffman, co-founder of LinkedIn, introduces his 'ABZ planning' framework for entrepreneurs to adapt in a constantly changing world. Everybody starts with 'Plan A' that begins in the present but looks ahead at the future. We want the plan to succeed and do everything in our power to make it so. Despite our efforts, this plan may not work. So, we turn to Plan B. However, an obstacle thwarts our intended strategy and requires us to pivot, and thus we shift to Plan Z – our best worst-case scenario, when we may need to jump on our lifeboat and regroup altogether.

Hoffman's framework is perfectly suited to business planning but can also be used to chart your professional or personal trajectories. The ABZ framework celebrates trial and error. Careers and businesses are iterative in nature because *life* itself is one such process. You may find that in a family business, the ABZ framework can serve you well. Plan A is your starting point, or where you presently find yourself. You have taken your strengths (or your firm's comparative advantage) into account and are trying to exploit them to achieve some kind of measurable success.

You may make some minor tweaks here and there along the way to fully optimize Plan A. Next comes Plan B. It is for when you reach an inflection point; you may need to change your methods to reach your goal, or maybe you need to change your goal altogether; perhaps you can now leverage the strengths of another family member. Regardless, you are still not too far from your original ideas laid out in Plan A; you have just had to pause, re-evaluate, and adjust to changing circumstances. Or perhaps you found a slightly new and better opportunity. Either way, you need not make a detailed plan for this scenario, but it is a good idea to think about your options. Finally, prepare your Plan Z. This is your reserve plan, your backup, your fallback. According to Hoffman, 'the certainty of a Plan Z backstop is what allows you to take on uncertainty and risk in your career.'[14] When Hoffman started his first company Socialnet, moving back in with his parents if things didn't work out was his Plan Z. This gave him the confidence to launch his business. Even if all else failed, he knew he wouldn't end up on the street.

Another example of the benefit of having a Plan Z comes from Harsh Mariwala, who leads Marico Ltd, an incredibly successful consumer goods family business. No stranger to failure, Mariwala explained in an interview, 'Whether it is the name, formulation, pricing, or packaging, every aspect of the merchandise plays a role in the success or failure of the product. In the prototype phase, instead of going for market research, you test your hypothesis among a group of people. For that, you should be willing to change things to innovate.'[15] Marico's Saffola Oil is associated with being healthy and is marketed as 'good for the heart'. The Marico team decided to leverage the brand's popularity among health-conscious consumers and launch a new product: baked snacks. The product did not end up taking off because, though healthy, it did not taste very good. When Mariwala makes mistakes, he admits it, but by being willing to regroup, backtrack, and try again, he ultimately finds the winning formula. In this case, it was to readjust and launch a breakfast cereal, Saffola Oats, which was able to capture a sizeable market share. Undeterred by failure, Mariwala knows that sometimes one has to pivot or start again, but as long as one is flexible and open to change, success is possible.

The father-son duo Ketan and Devang Jhaveri is the force behind the luxury designer brand Devotie. Devang, a driven and articulate young man, left a great impression on me the first time I met him. At the time, he shared his experience of building a global brand along with his father. For the first several years, after the company was founded, they were constantly adapting to changing fashion trends. In the beginning, Devotie manufactured men's jewellery but two years into this venture, the trend changed, and men were no longer wearing rings, pendants, and chains as much. Devang and his father had to course-correct.

They focused on their primary strengths – product design and development – and started developing products such as watches, shoes, and leather goods. This helped them remain relevant and grow despite the rapidly changing fashion market.

Mudit Mohini applied a similar thought process at Delhi Press as she led her business from magazines into books, moving on to schoolbooks, and later into digitized learning platforms for schools. When I spoke to Mudit, she explained, 'As magazines are losing their relevance in India and people are reading more on WhatsApp, I decided to change the format of our most loved children's magazine *Champak* into a class-wise magazine which schools could prescribe to inculcate the habit of reading. This was very well received by schools and increased our reading base tremendously.' This type of tweaking along the way, as Mudit learned from experience and grew her business, has helped her ensure that her business and products remain relevant in the publishing industry.

In the steel industry, project-management companies (PMCs) are the link between the client, the architect, the supplier, and the site contractor. PMCs today hire 'expeditors' whose sole purpose is to troubleshoot unforeseen issues, fix delays, and smooth out kinks as the project progresses. These expeditors are jugaadus by another name. They provide on-the-spot solutions, usually have few resources to work with, and must always be ready with alternative plans to fall back on. A lead expeditor could easily be designated as a 'manager of jugaad'. PMCs have not only embraced the use of jugaad, but have also standardized its use. An expeditor bears a Swiss Army knife, regularly correcting their course, adapting, and relying on the armour of their team to get past all the hurdles.

One should always keep moving, both in business and in life – that tells us we are still in the game. Plans from A to Y may fail, but one still has Plan Z – the final option. If Plan Z is stable and marked out, it may give you the space to revisit plans A and B and take on the risk that comes with them. A good leader is flexible, open to change, and ready to deploy alternatives in this manner.

The Emergency Parachute: How to Take the Leap

Life is not always linear, and things do not need to happen in the order in which they were planned. Jugaad tells us that sometimes you have to jump off the plane *and then* figure out how to open the parachute. If you succeed, terrific, but if you fail, you had nothing to lose in the first place!

To have an emergency parachute in the survival toolkit is to have a carefully packed safety net so that we can take the leap into the unknown. Quite literally, working in a family business may feel like you are jumping off a plane from way above the clouds with very little visibility. You have no idea how deep the drop is. Who knows how the landing will be. Fast or slow, rocky or smooth. But what the parachute ensures is that we will, for sure, land, often right back on our feet and be wiser for it. But we have to take the leap, for no good will come if we do not move. So, the parachute becomes our protector, our invisible guardian, convincing us that we will regret not doing something at all much more than doing it incorrectly.

The emergency parachute embodies:
1. The do-or-die spirit
2. The 'just do it' motto

Do or die!

Transformational change is driven by a strong urge for immediate change in the status quo. Whether within an organization or in yourself, the desire to change is fundamental to getting the ball rolling, without which you may risk institutional, organizational, or personal stagnation. Instead of waiting for the right opportunity to come your way, ignite the spark of change in yourself. Of course, things will get stressful – sometimes stress means you are closer to your goals – but you will be astounded by the creativity that comes with it. When time is running out, your mind goes into overdrive to get you to the finish line. You will come up with new ideas and innovative solutions and maybe even do the impossible. Simply put, when you want to change, begin the countdown and get ready to do or die.

Say you are locked in a room with three people. You start to see smoke from the hallway creeping into the room under the door, indicating that a fire is raging outside. If you do nothing, you will surely suffocate and die from the smoke, or eventually, the fire will reach you. But if you come together as a team – ignited by the urgency of the situation – you will find a creative way to escape, given that the situation calls for a fight-or-flight response. Your survival instinct will kick in as you will have no other option in front of you. With no time to brainstorm or ruminate, you will realize you need to prioritize and act swiftly and efficiently. You may start running towards the stairs, consider going to the fire exit with a chute, or even jumping out of the window – you *will* do something to save your life.

This example gives a sense of how important urgency is for the process of innovation. When you are bound by time or resources, the 'do-or-die' spirit needs to be activated to compel you to think outside of the box.

At a guest lecture at the Tata Institute of Social Sciences, where I was speaking about how to run a successful startup, a student raised his hand and said, 'I have a good business idea. But I don't know where to start.' Immediately there were murmurs of agreement around the room. I explained truthfully that there was no such thing as the correct starting point and that each student or idea might require different pathways. If they were stuck, I suggested, they could try a few different options to get the ball rolling.

- Make use of the internet to see what's out there in terms of supply and demand for your product/service.
- Start working on a website for your product/service using a free web tool.
- Launch a survey to understand market needs and send it to everyone in your team.
- Start mailing suppliers and vendors inquiring about product specification and prices.
- Look at job portals for the required and relevant skills associated with your business idea.

The more you analyze your proposed product or service, the more questions you will have; eventually these will lead you to more answers. The harder you work, the luckier you get. And when you finally make the jump, you have nothing to lose because a whole host of opportunities await you.

John Kotter, Emeritus Professor of Leadership at Harvard Business School, discusses in his book *A Sense of Urgency* why humans find it hard to adapt to change – in ourselves, our habits, or our actions – and what we can do to fix this. Kotter talks about how the issue of urgency plagues us all, especially as part of a group. He warns that when groups of people (for example, business firms) mishandle the challenges that emerge during a time of urgency, there can be significant negative consequences. However, those who succeed in handling these challenges will be better equipped for future success, no matter the endeavour they choose to pursue.

Kotter asserts, 'At the very beginning of any effort to make changes of any magnitude if [the] sense of urgency is not high enough and complacency is not low enough, everything else becomes so much more difficult.'[16] Furthermore, he contends that most of us are completely oblivious to complacency, which makes efforts to bring about change more complicated. Ironically, although success requires change, success can also make us complacent. But if we are not ready to change with the world around us, we will not be able to achieve any more success.

Addressing the misconception that urgency is more ubiquitous and harmful than complacency, Kotter states that to him, urgency is not about being frantic, something that only brings chaos and dysfunction. A false sense of urgency is also not conducive to growth and change because it fosters an environment of 'anxiety, anger, and frustration'.[17] But by being thoughtful and decisive during moments of urgency, individuals and organizations will be prepared to brace themselves against unexpected hiccups or roadblocks when the frenzy finally dies down.

According to Kotter, change is 'continuous', and there is simply no time to get lazy. Life now turns on a dime, so businesses need to be equipped with the right toolkit to respond thoughtfully and reasonably. In the past, when change was more of an intermittent occurrence, organizations would find it difficult to foster a sense of urgency because a drastic change was required only sporadically. It is easy to take urgency for granted in today's era of 'continuous' change. But in reality, sustaining elevated levels of urgency has become the new challenge.

Just do it!

In Reid Hoffman's *The Startup of You*, he talks about the idea of serendipity and how it manifests only when we are not sedentary. When one is constantly moving about and looking for challenges, one invites new opportunities. Similarly, Hoffman discusses the concept of 'serendipitous network intelligence' that makes opportunities turn up at your doorstep through frequent and continuous engagements of personal and professional networks. Examples include a seemingly out-of-the-blue email from a friend you had not heard from in a while, or a job lead from a former colleague. Keeping your eyes and ears open will allow opportunities to flow your way.

A sense of speed and urgency is crucial in a world that never sleeps. Millions of new ideas are tried and tested every day; some are successful and some end up as failures. New companies are launched while others are forced to shutter their doors. The scale and speed at which information can now be gathered, organized, and shared require those who want to succeed to adapt quickly. Without including speed in your toolkit, you will not be able to keep up in a race that grows more and more competitive with the advance of globalization. Else you run the risk of your idea, your business, and even you simply being left behind. I want to bring in some more of Tina Fey's wisdom here. Quoting her boss at *Saturday Night Live*, Lorne Michaels, she writes, 'The show doesn't go on because it's ready; it goes on because it's 11:30.'[18] You can try to fine-tune and polish over and over, but at some point, you have to just let it go and jump into action.

I want to share an example from our family business that touches upon this idea. We had spent many months considering adding a civil engineering division to our business, which would mean we could do all the flooring and civil footing for our building projects. This meant adding another department and also making the process much easier for the client. We could come in right at the ground-levelling stage and give the client an end-to-end solution for their building. We talked about this idea endlessly as a family and as a business but never got around to it.

Then, as it happened, one of our clients stipulated that they would only award a contract to a company that could provide both civil and steel services as they did not want to deal with two separate contractors. At that point, we had not implemented our idea, but the client wanted exactly that. We wanted to win the contract and realized everything we had been discussing for months had to be implemented overnight. The client's demands lit a fire under us!

We hurried to recruit a civil engineering team and build a proposal for the client. We won the bid, and this is how our civil works division was born. We quickly mobilized our team to meet our client's needs, thanks in part to the sense of urgency that brought out the 'do-or-die' spirit and we decided to 'just do it'. We worked harder than ever to ensure our first composite contract would serve as a good reference for future bids. Our client (an Italian cement company) valued our quality and efficiency and went on to award us more such contracts. Since then, we have institutionalized a civil engineering division and worked on other composite steel and civil projects in tandem.

The idea had been playing on our minds for years, but the impetus to move forward was an external countdown created (unknowingly) by our client. As we have discussed previously, intrinsic motivation is admirable, but hard to muster. It is difficult to create a sense of urgency for ourselves without adequate reason, as we usually end up making excuses for inaction. However, when circumstances change outside of our control, we have no choice but to act. When such an opportunity comes knocking, it is not the time to recoil or retreat. Instead, it is an opportunity to learn and grow, refresh, and reinvent. When that moment comes, recognize it, respond to it, and get to it.

We have now gone through the tools in our survival kit. By now, you should have a grasp of how and when to use them. With the multipurpose hat, the flashlight, the superhero cape, the Swiss Army knife, and the parachute, you can tackle each new day knowing you are more ready than ever to confront the challenges you may face in your business.

सुते के पाड्डे जाम

Sutte ke padde jamme

(You snooze, you lose)

This pithy Haryanvi quote, often repeated by my father, best captures the essence of urgency. In Haryana, a *padda* is a buffalo, and a *paddi* its female counterpart. Since paddis produce milk, they are an important source of income for villagers. On the other hand, a padda is pretty much useless to the villagers. The story goes something like this: Two neighbours in a village owned a cow each. Both animals got pregnant and as luck would have it, each was due to deliver around the same time – an unexpected but auspicious sign. As the due date inched closer, both neighbours took different approaches. Kalu was the very definition of vigilant; he kept guard over his precious cow day and night. He did not want to miss the birth of the calf at all. Across the street, Kalu's neighbour Bholu was more or less indifferent. He was lazy and disinterested and napped whenever he could. It came as no surprise that he paid little attention to his cow, never bothering to check on her as the birth drew near.

Finally, on the due date, both the cows gave birth at the same time in the late hours of the night, almost as if they had made a pact between themselves. Of course,

Kalu was by the side of his cow, while Bholu was fast asleep, completely oblivious to the atmosphere of excitement just a few metres from where he slept. Kalu's cow birthed a male calf, while lazy Bholu's gave birth to the ultimate prize, a paddi. Needless to say, the attentive Kalu was crestfallen about the outcome. But Kalu did not let disappointment consume him. The cunning man that he was, he turned the situation to his benefit. With only a few hours to act, Kalu immediately sprang into action and decided to switch the calves, knowing Bholu would be none the wiser come morning.

The next day, the two neighbours met for a cup of tea. As expected, Bholu let out a deep sigh and complained that his buffalo gave birth to a padda. Kalu, suppressing a smile, consoled his neighbour and said to himself, '*Sutte ke padde jamme.*'

Wallowing and complaining if we were stuck in a less-than-ideal situation, or when simply confronted by a case of bad luck, is futile. Instead, remember to be vigilant. If there is sufficient will and motivation (buoyed by preparedness), an individual can take fate into their own hands and make their own success. In short, this folk tale teaches us to keep our eyes open and grab any opportunity that comes our way.

5

SURVIVING RISK AND FAILURE

THE SURVIVAL KIT CAN EQUIP FAMILY BUSINESSES FOR success, but every experienced business owner is aware that the path to success is neither smooth nor linear. Although using these tools to polish your business practices will certainly mitigate the challenges and prepare you for the difficult road ahead, it is important to remember that both risk and failures are to be expected in your personal and professional journey. Therefore, you should not be running away from them. In fact, at times, facing obstacles head on is the best way to get closer to success. Only when you don't fear risk and failure, and instead look at them as learning opportunities, can you discover an entirely new set of possibilities. It will take practice, but you will find it becomes easier with time. In other words, you will learn that the only way out of challenges is to simply confront them. Going around them will not work; such methods will only delay the inevitable. But by diving straight in, you will learn a lot about yourself and develop critical life skills that will enable you to succeed in the future.

This goes for me too. I have strived to incorporate these tools in my life, but I often veer off the path because of unexpected obstacles, change in plans, and failures. Such moments can be frustrating. But at the same time, because I am armed with my survival kit, I feel better prepared to confront such obstacles when they arise. I have grown more confident and less fearful of what is to come. And not every moment in life requires the application of these tools; it is important to recognize the uniqueness of your situation and decide what works for you and what doesn't. There isn't a one-size-fits-all solution to life. It is only through experience, intuition, and practice that one learns what works best for you.

My family immigrated to Mumbai from Haryana in the early 1990s. As I learn more and more about where my family comes from, I have realized that Haryana's cultural heritage deserves and requires national attention, especially since it is at the risk of vanishing. Haryana has its own dialect, Haryanvi, which is similar to Hindi in sound and script, but louder and full of gusto. Haryanvi embodies its people's fierce attitude, their ability to say things without holding back, their implicit sarcasm, and the sheer wisdom of their crassness. Haryanvi has unique proverbs and sayings that highlight valuable life lessons with a touch of humour. Haryanvi folk tales, stories, and jokes have been passed down in my family across more than five generations.

In Haryanvi culture, failure is quickly forgotten – it's all water under the bridge. Life is too short to dwell on what could have been, and thus, being thick-skinned is a part of the culture. Haryanvis grow up learning how to be tough and to keep moving ahead, no matter what happens, from a very young age. Failure, risk, and conflict are mere speedbumps, not roadblocks. If a child falls and skins his knee, he does not cry; he picks himself up and keeps playing. Haryanvi folklore offers lessons about living a no-nonsense, 'pull-yourself-up-by-your-bootstraps' life. These lessons are instilled from a young age and shape our personal and professional trajectories.

हरयाणवी भूखा रह सकता है, बोले बिना नहीं रह सकता।
Haryanvi bhookha reh sakta hai, bole bina nahi reh sake
(A Haryanvi can go without food, but cannot go without speaking his or her mind)

My father regularly applied dozens of memorable Haryanvi adages at work and shared them with us at home. They are so deeply ingrained in me that I have begun to apply them myself. They add a sense of levity to my life and sometimes help put into words what I face in my personal and professional lives. They also remind me of the concepts of jugaad I have incorporated in my life over the years. They have thus allowed me to look beyond the obstacles I have faced and are an essential part of my personal survival toolkit.

At some point or another, all generations involved in a family business experience anxieties, fears, conflicts, and failure irrespective of age, gender, title, or salary. For example, the first-generation entrepreneur who has to cede control to the next generation but is not sure whether the latter can handle the business. Or perhaps the next-generation leader terrified of making a wrong decision and embarrassing their parents and leading the family business to failure.

Similarly, what counts as a success for one can be perceived differently by another. When it comes to a family business, several moving parts make the dynamics of risk and failure more complex. But once we have our toolkit in place, we use our *multipurpose hat* to switch between roles; shine the light on what matters with our *flashlight*; wear our *superhero cape* and be courageous; fix our problems with the *Swiss Army knife*; and fasten our *parachutes* to simply 'do'.

In this chapter, I share the wisdom of the Haryanvi adages I have added to my toolkit which offer valuable insights into how to survive the risks and failures faced by many family businesses. These short stories and witty sayings hold important management lessons which have assisted me in running my business and will help you do the same. There are some emotions that we, the next gens, have all felt recurrently in our family business. In extreme circumstances, these emotions have reached a breaking point and we have also considered quitting our family business altogether. That is why, in the following section, I have addressed these emotions head-on and offered Haryanvi wisdom to help us deal with them. For each negative emotion, we can think of a Haryanvi saying to help add perspective and provide us with the positivity we need.

Fear

'मैं डर गया क्यूँकि कोई कोनी था |'
'जब कोई कोनी था तो डरया क्यूं भाई?'

'Mai dar gaya kyunki koyi koni tha.'
'Jab koi koni tha toh darya kyun bhai?'

'I was afraid because there was no one there!'
'But, dude, if there really was no one,
who were you afraid of?'

This idiom has a short Haryanvi tale behind it. A young man is walking on an empty road at night. Upon reaching home, he tells his father that he was afraid to be alone on the road. His father responds by saying that he was, in effect, safer alone than he would have been if a suspicious person had been walking along with him.

This saying can be applied to other situations: When we delay taking a decision or become indecisive out of fear. Or when nervousness mars our judgement and we spiral into anxiety. Sometimes, fear makes us imagine the worst which hinders our ability to act.

The most common stereotype about the next-gen members of a family business is that they are arrogant and overconfident, and expect everything to come easily to them. But the reality is that these Gen Y and Z members become overwhelmed with self-doubt over joining the family business. They have witnessed their parents working hard for years and feel immense pressure to perform as well or even better than their parents, which leads them to wonder whether they can truly deliver what is expected of them. Furthermore, all eyes are on them (both within the company and in the local community).

A bit of nervousness is natural when venturing beyond one's comfort zone, more so when one's family name is on the line. Not having a clear roadmap to success can bring even more anxiety. But the younger generation must understand that *all* generations deal with anxiety. Given the differences in experiences, each person deals with it differently.

The younger generation is often not well equipped to know how to move on – some shut out all advice, some lash out at others, others play the blame game. Moreover, anxiety is hardly discussed within a family business context, which makes it even more debilitating. Anxiety, associated with depression and medication, is thought to be something only the 'weak' experience. Space must be created within family businesses to allow an open discussion of feelings. Despite the universal nature of fear and anxiety, the younger generation faces the greatest challenge in addressing their fears given their lack of experience in confronting failure. Fear should serve to push, not paralyze. You must take control of the situation and empower yourself.

Anu Aga, one of India's wealthiest women, also experienced fear when she had to take over the reins of her husband's company, Thermax Ltd, after her husband passed away unexpectedly. Describing her experience, she said, 'I just wasn't ready. I kept devaluing myself and thought that I was only being invited to take over because we as a family own this business. I really felt miserable, missing my husband, yet, having to assume his role ... I didn't know hardcore business, and I was terrible at finance. Being at the helm of the capital goods industry, I had to know both.'[1] She feared she wouldn't be up to the challenge. What did she do then? She turned to mindfulness, surrounded herself with experts and employees who could guide her and showed vulnerability. She could have let fear consume her, but instead, she faced it head-on. She pushed past her fear, donned her superhero cape, and ended up becoming incredibly successful.

As a next-gen member, how do you cut through your fear and anxiety? For members of the Y and Z generations, joining the family business poses unique challenges as compared to other firms. In *Next Generation Success*, family business expert John Davis shares how after extensive conversations with senior and junior members of family businesses he concluded that the younger generation is primarily concerned with 'demonstrating that they can one day lead the company'[2]. In other words, they want to prove (either to themselves and/or to their families) that they are indeed capable of success.

In the following example, we will examine the situation of a younger generation that wants the support of a senior member to launch a new venture.

Binoy is a second-generation member of a family business that focuses on fruit and vegetable trading in India. His father, Amrit, has grown the business exponentially over the years and is heavily involved in its day-to-day operations. While Amrit had little in the way of formal education, his son studied in a private school and then went on to graduate with an MBA from an American university. Binoy wants to contribute to the business's growth and has been researching the industry. After studying industry papers and based on his experience, he concludes that trading in organic fruits and vegetables will become the latest fast-growing trend. He believes that getting into the organic market will be beneficial for the business and wants to bring the idea to his father. What does he need to do to get his father's approval? Similarly, what can Amrit do to support his son's ambitions?

- **Sell the plan**: Binoy needs to create a detailed proposal, just as he would if he were trying to pitch an idea to someone outside his family. He needs to display a strong understanding of the market he would like to penetrate or the trends he wants to exploit, which takes into consideration factors such as the competition, potential threats, regulatory challenges, and the firm's unique selling point. The proposal should also incorporate personal factors. Family businesses tend to be more traditional and risk-averse, so Binoy needs to assure his father that the new venture will not disrupt or cannibalize the existing business. In this case, the foray into the organic market could be a spin-off or subsidiary.

- **Start small**: Family businesses are often more fiscally conservative than their corporate counterparts. When an entrepreneurial venture by a next-gen family member is to be invested in, the business is likely to be even more cautious. Binoy should present the plan as a small, viable, and calculated risk. The younger generation tends to dream big and is unwilling to compromise to a small pilot, but by demonstrating restraint, Binoy can convince his father to test the waters.

- **Consider the timing**: Ideas and dreams rarely come at the perfect time. Sometimes, you may have to think about an idea for years before it begins to take shape and materialize. If Amrit says no the first time, Binoy should remain patient and wait for a more optimal time to present his idea again.

- **Prepare for the worst**: Binoy needs to understand his father's point of view too. What if the venture fails? He needs to plan for the eventuality that the venture ends up as a loss. What will he do to try and earn the money back? By preparing for this possibility, Binoy will show his father that he is being practical and has thought about all the possibilities.

- **Do the research**: The younger generation is often more keyed into trends that the older generation may not have even have heard of. But just because Amrit has not heard of the organic food trend does not mean that people will not be interested in it. By doing his research, Binoy can prove his drive, awareness, and commitment. It will also help Binoy craft a measured response to any questions his father may throw at him.

- **Look to connections**: Even if Amrit feels like he cannot support his son's organic venture, he does not have to shut the door completely. Perhaps he has friends or connections who might be willing to partner with his son. By providing him with other avenues, he can show his son that while he cannot launch the venture through his own business, he still supports his son's entrepreneurial ambitions and will do whatever he can to support Binoy.

- **Examine the budget**: Just as Binoy needs to be flexible with the budget he may receive, so should Amrit if he says yes. There needs to be a careful examination of the current financial situation of the business to determine how much money can be risked. With careful auditing, Amrit can respond to his son and explain how much money is available and why he cannot fund Binoy's venture – a better response than simply claiming that there are no funds.

- **Be mindful of your response**: Sometimes, your child may come to you with a suggestion that you are convinced will not work. In such a case, you need to be careful about how you communicate your reservations. Scoffing at the idea can discourage your child from bringing new ideas to you in the future. Take the time to craft a measured response in a calm tone, explaining the issues you see in the proposal and inviting them to find ways to overcome or address them. Crushing the dream outright will only lead to resentment and may also cause them to blindly pursue the venture once they have the reins of the business.

Those in Amrit's generation should strive to maintain a balance with their juniors. On one hand, the younger generation wants more responsibility and independence, and to be treated like adults who can run a business. On the other, given the parent-child dynamic, they easily slip back into their role as the child who wants their dreams and aspirations to be validated by the parent. In this case study, Binoy needs to put himself in his father's shoes and consider the concerns, risks, and fears his father may have in relation to a new venture. In turn, Amrit needs to balance his desire to support his son and his responsibility to do what is right for the business.

Indifference

तेरी मेरी बनै कोनी, तेरे बिना सरै कोनी।

Teri meri bane koni, tere bina sare koni
(Can't live with you, can't live without you)

This idiom reminds us that there will always be people in our life and business with whom we are in constant conflict, but at the same time, cannot exist without. Learn to co-exist with such individuals who are important to you or your business, even if you do not agree with them. Imagine for a moment that your mother-in-law – who you do not get along with – is significantly involved in the day-to-day operations of your family business. You desperately wish she would just disappear and get her nose out of your work life. However, every time you have a board meeting, she contributes some excellent ideas and insights that you have seen improve business operations. You might think you would be much better off without her around, but in fact, these important contributions are worth the frustration.

It took me all my twenties and a large part of my thirties to develop a genuine sense of empathy. This lack of empathy had made me rather cold-hearted, and I am ashamed to admit this. When I was younger, I was determined to prove myself at all costs. I believed that if I were to be taken seriously, I had to remain tough (which sometimes translated to being insensitive). Being the lone woman in my work ecosystem, I was convinced that any 'soft' behaviour would lead the all-male staff to consider me to be 'emotional' and hence 'weak'. So, I pursued work with a no-nonsense and stern attitude. I came off as rude and mean at times, oblivious about the impact of my actions on the people around me, and in particular, the staff members I worked with. Many times, I was insensitive to the needs of my fellow female staff members who were juggling home, children, in-laws, and work. I had only myself to take care of, so I gave little thought to appreciating how much additional work women around me had to do even before they arrived in the morning. And worst of all, I felt everyone was dispensable, that I could do anyone's share of the work if they were to leave. My father would often remind me to consider that while I may not be able to tolerate some of my co-workers, I wouldn't survive without them at work for even one day. It took several events and as many failures for me to develop a sense of empathy and humility in this regard.

One such moment of learning presented itself to me after I gave birth to my first child. I struggled to return to work, given the new demands on my body, my mind, and my time. Maternity leave made me feel redundant; my efficiency and focus were lagging; and I was behind in the new technologies we had adopted at work. As I started to grow out of my youthful ignorance and over confidence, I realized just how difficult it was for so many of us to leave behind the responsibilities of the home and come to work.

Mudit Mohini also shared with me how her entry into her family business was a rocky one, since it was always perceived that she would only last until she was married. She explained, 'It was not easy for everyone to accept that women can continue working with their fathers while married and living in her "husband's house."' Upon joining, she received a very cold welcome. But Mudit persevered and let her passion for books (and later children's books) guide her along the way. She carved a path and a role for herself and made herself an irreplaceable part of the management team.

With time and experience, I decided to approach my work and my co-workers with a more understanding outlook. My responses grew more thoughtful as opposed to reactionary. I am now able to maintain my composure and acknowledge that my anxiety was at the root of some of my hasty actions. Though I had unfortunately missed out on many opportunities to connect with my team members and do well by them, I was grateful for this eventual lesson in empathy which continues to help me to this day.

Empathy helps us build strong bonds with others, creates a culture of understanding, and demonstrates acceptance of differences. By working on being empathetic to others, you can be a more effective and approachable leader who has their employees' trust and respect. Remember to use your flashlight to focus on how others may feel or be affected, and prioritize ubuntu above all.

False Confidence

बुआ जाऊँ जाऊँ करैथी, फूफा लेण आगया

Bua jau jau kare thi, fufa len aa gaya
(The aunt threatened to leave only to find her bluff being called)

When we are faking something, sometimes the universe calls our bluff and puts us to the test to reveal our true colours. We often hatch clever plans, thinking we can outsmart those around us. However, we are often proven wrong and our supposed plans come back to bite us. As such, we may err on the side of projecting a sense of overconfidence or arrogance to compensate for this unexpected turn of events. A Haryanvi folk tale about a couple illustrates this beautifully.

Jalebi and Laddoo Ram had been married for two years and lived at Laddoo Ram's parents' house in Sirsa. One day, Jalebi got into a heated argument with her husband and stormed out of the house. She yelled that she was returning to her parents' home in Bhiwani, three hours away from Sirsa. But Jalebi quickly grew bored of Bhiwani. Jalebi's parents were glad to have her home but always bickered with her since she threatened them daily by saying she would go back to Sirsa. Unsurprisingly, this frustrated her parents to no end.

But even though Jalebi had no intention of returning to Sirsa just yet, an unexpected visitor turned up at her parents' door. Her husband had arrived without notice and apologized profusely, asking Jalebi to return home with him. Caught off guard and unwilling to go back on her threat to her parents, Jalebi had no choice but to swallow her pride and dutifully return to Sirsa.

Jalebi was not serious about acting on her threat, but under the changed circumstances she was caught between maintaining her pride and sacrificing her ego. She had to make a choice on the spot. She may have thought herself to be clever, but her story tells us the universe had a different idea in mind.

We can observe many similar examples in the professional world. For instance, imagine you are frustrated with your father who runs your family business. You come up with a plan to make your father believe that you would quit the job if you did not get your way at work. You assume you will get him to listen and get to stay because you are irreplaceable as a family member. So, one day, you turn up at your father's cabin and threaten that if he did not support your decisions, you would resign immediately. You may think the threat will leave your father with only one option: to give in because you are indispensable to the company. Much to your surprise, your father calls your bluff and asks you to leave. You leave the meeting wondering what just happened. You clearly don't want out.

When we let our ego take over, it blinds us. We start thinking we are infallible, but we are often proved wrong. We are usually better served by being humble, forthcoming, and direct. This is difficult in the face of risk or failure, but it is an important lesson. Our word is our bond, and we must be fully prepared to keep our promises because the universe will test us to see if we can do so. In the business world, this lesson is especially important given the tight margins small businesses operate within and the risks they often have to take.

If a business operates on a model of higher risks through threats and deceit, it may be forced to backtrack if the universe (via a customer, a competitor, the market, or a regulator) intervenes and calls its bluff. Conversely, if a business operates on the model of honesty, humility, and transparent communication, it will thrive and be able to benefit from calculated risks. To sum up, confidence is important, but feigned overconfidence will not help you avert risk or failure.

Frustration

सौ सुनार की एक लुहार की

Sau sunaar ki ek luhar ki
(A single strike of the blacksmith's hammer is far more impactful than a hundred small strikes of the goldsmith's)

Each situation calls for a solution specific to the problem. You cannot expect a goldsmith to work with a sturdy metal like iron. Sometimes one decisive and strong action can be better than many small, incremental efforts. There are times in business when turnover and profits can be anxiety-inducing for all generations. One may be doing the right things to drive revenue, but there may not be significant profits to show for it. Roma Bakshani, executive director of BNT Connections, went through a similar situation a decade ago. She was working hard and trying everything to turn her business around. They were bagging orders, executing them, introducing new technology, trying every trick in the book. But the numbers just weren't improving fast enough. My father calls this 'drinking soup with a fork'– you may churn the soup with the spoon, but none of it is getting to your lips if you use a fork to consume it. It is immensely frustrating.

Around 2010 the retail industry had taken a downward turn and garment manufacturing, a labour-intensive business, was operating on slim margins. 'At times the only avenue for profit was the government subsidy support,' Roma told me. So, when they were presented with a buyer who would take over their set-up and their employees, Roma was both exhausted and apprehensive. Initially, she felt that she had let her business down, failed at keeping her father's dream going. However, she was able to also analyze objectively that this wasn't her fault and that running a huge team of 2,500 workers with such low competitive prices was no way to run a business. Roma was both brave and astute to help make the right call for her business. All the small efforts, akin to a goldsmith at work, were going nowhere and so a big bold step, kind of like a blacksmith's blow, was needed to shake things up.

In business, the bottlenecks are not always obvious. When you start feeling as if you are indeed drinking soup with a fork, it is easy for failure and fatigue to seep in. In times like these, it is critical to get to the root of the problem and consider a correction in course; think about the Swiss Army knife in your toolkit and see how you can make adjustments. There is no shame in slowing down, shutting some production lines, or asking stakeholders for help. Without profits, and cash in your bank account, the business will not survive. Instead, focus on quality and on widening the gap between sales and costs, not just on the revenue. Big looks good, but cash is king.

As we've noted earlier, adaptability has an important role to play in our approach to business. As we progress in our professional lives, it is easy to get comfortable in our ways, especially when things are going well. Because of this, we may not be inspired to get to the root of problems when things don't go the way we planned, or maybe we simply won't know how to solve the issue.

Adaptability and the jugaad mindset will motivate you to step back and try to consider the situation from a different perspective. Your Swiss Army knife will help you fix the chinks in your armour with which you will be able to steel yourself against the fatigue and frustration that come with failure. But only if you recognize that missteps and obstacles are all part of the game and acknowledge the huge number of resources you have at your disposal (for example, your networks) can you build an armour ahead of time.

In leveraging your armour, don't forget to reach out for help within and outside your family. For over three decades, my father has received help from businessmen from Haryana and his network of friends in Mumbai. Similarly, I too have benefited greatly thanks to influential personalities who have provided mobility and access that were far beyond my reach and have helped me get out of ruts. My favourite professor in college went above and beyond to support me during my classes, internships, and research. Through my professors, I had the opportunity to travel everywhere: from Milledgeville, Georgia to Sydney, Australia. Our suppliers have worked their schedules around to help us with the spare parts that we needed urgently. Our clients have valued our honesty and have been considerate when shipments got delayed. I have found that strong personal or professional connections can have a tremendous impact on your life and your success. Especially in times of frustration, these connections can provide that outside perspective you need the most. Though you can achieve quite a bit of success by gathering support from the ground up, you can reach your goals a whole lot faster by standing on the shoulders of giants.

Control

कटै जाट का, सीखै नाई का

Kate jaat ka, seekhe naai ka

(While the barber's son hones his skills, it's the customer who risks a bad haircut)

Say you hire a firm to come in and fix some machines, and the firm conducts several trial-and-error experiments to figure out what went wrong. But all this while, you are being billed by the firm. In such a situation, it is important to analyze how much you are willing to spend, and how many such experiments you will allow them to carry out, given that you are the one having to bear the costs and loss of profit from the breakdown.

My father loves to use the aforementioned Haryanvi phrase on me. He says he has had to bear the costs of all my experiential learning, miscalculations, and errors. Unsurprisingly, most mistakes in family businesses come at a cost, and it is usually the older generation that has to foot the bill. This can often frustrate, disillusion, anger, or disappoint them. Though costly, this process is also an important part of the younger generation's personal and professional development. By allowing the younger generation some wiggle room and a sense of autonomy, the older generation can create a space that enables the younger generation to thrive and grow into successful business leaders. If the older generation does not grant their progeny autonomy and a chance to spread their wings, they turn into 'helicopter parents' who hinder creativity and innovation.

The older generation must remember that experimentation and independence are inevitably adjoined to failure. It is precisely this failure that will lead to the younger generation's success. Future leaders need to make mistakes while they still have the support, backing, and protection of their elders so that they can avert or deal with failure when their turn comes. The younger generation may make a rash investment, fail to do the required research on a new market or trend, or sign a bad deal. But while it may cost a bit now, the older generation must remember the returns will be substantial down the road.

Fear of Failure

घी खिंडा दिया तो क्या हुआ, गया तो खिचड़ी में ही ना

Ghee khinda diya toh kya hua, gaya toh khichdi mein hi na
(If you spill some extra butter into the food while
cooking, what's so terrible about it?)

This adage tells us that no effort goes in vain. Everything we do – as long as it's intentional and in good faith – is important and something we can learn from on our journey of personal and professional development. Though it might be hard to believe, steel and ghee are similar in some ways. It is hard to screw up with steel; its very nature makes it difficult to waste given how easy it is to recycle and reuse this metal. Similarly, adding a bit too much or too little ghee does not ruin a meal either.

Mistakes make for valuable learning experiences. Do not be so hard on yourself when you slip – you may just end up with an accidental masterpiece. My mother has instilled in us the self-assurance we rely on whenever we are faced with doubt. For instance, my father reprimands his team quite fiercely when they screw up, but always ends up regretting doing so. When he tells my mother about it, she assures him that his teammates do understand where he was coming from and why he was angry. While being so tough on them may not have been entirely right, it does not hurt to scare them a little more than needed so that they are more cautious next time.

My father often quotes this adage when I make mistakes on our factory floor. On one occasion, we invested time, effort, and resources to produce material for a client who never paid us for it. I learned the hard way to wait for the advance payment before I begin production. Thankfully, my father has shown me that steel can be reused for other projects, so it was not a total waste. Mistakes are part of the learning process. And with every mistake, one grows that much closer to being the best leader one can be. The flashlight (understanding) and the superhero cape (guts) come into play here. 'Understanding' means to learn and absorb as much as possible. Put in the work to understand your industry, company, or product as deeply as you can. Combine it with 'guts' – that is passion, energy, and fearlessness – and you get a winning combo.

Remember that having both understanding and guts does not mean you will not fail. What it does mean, however, is that you will have empowered yourself to succeed. You have done everything to put yourself on the path to success. Those around you, such as your parents in the business, will see the effort, dedication, and motivation you have thrown into your work. Mistakes that you make will therefore not be judged as harshly. Why? Because you prepared as well as you could. You did the work. And you did it with conviction. It is easier to reprimand someone for their mistake if they did not give it their all. But if you give it your everything that makes all the difference.

Dejection

यो के कुंभ का मेला सै जो बारा साल बाद आवेगा

Yo ke Kumbh ka mela se jo barah saal baad aavega
(You will get a second chance sooner than you think)

The famous Hindu festival, the Kumbh Mela, is celebrated over the course of twelve years and is observed in rotation at four sacred sites in India. Our lives, however, are not premeditated as the Kumbh. Time always moves forward, but that does not mean that our past will dictate the future. You may stumble along the path, or you may fall. You might miss deadlines, your plans may get derailed, your contracts may fall through, and your clients may be disappointed. But that does not mean that you will not get a chance to make amends, or that you will have to wait forever to get an opportunity again. As we gather more experience, knowledge, and wisdom, we become better versions of ourselves every single day. If something in the past did not quite work out – perhaps a new job, project, or business – do not let its failure dictate what happens next. You can, and you must, try again.

In chapter 4, I discussed the concept of ABZ planning, which allows you to try, fail, and eventually succeed. Your original idea or how you currently operate is plan A. You tweak it as required, but business typically proceeds as usual. When you hit a roadblock, or during a churn, it is time to bring out Plan B. This could be an overhaul of Plan A, or perhaps a new project or idea that is tangentially related to A but will be more fruitful. When all fails, you turn to Plan Z, an unfailing, reliable, and certain solution. Z is your ultimate backup plan in case of an emergency, to keep you going until you discover a new Plan A.

Yash Dongre, designer Anita Dongre's son and Business Head, House of Anita Dongre, had to deal with the Covid-19 setback in the retail industry. Stores had to be shut down for close to three months. Thankfully, they had an existing online presence and Yash was quick to adjust his efforts and grab the second chance he saw in front of him. 'We put our whole energy there; we strengthened our business within the online space, started bringing in more technology partners to improve our customer experience, and we've been seeing a very healthy growth in our e-commerce numbers.'[4]

Regret

मैं समझूंगी की एक टायर फट गया।

Mai samjhungi ki ek tyre phat gaya
(I'll just take it to mean that a tyre burst)
– Darshana Gupta

My father also owns a transport and logistics company that takes care of internal raw material movement for large, integrated steel plants. His assets in this business are heavy-duty earth-moving equipment such as dumper trucks, excavators, wheel loaders, and cranes. These vehicles undergo incredible wear and tear day after day. Often, while mining a mineral or bringing iron ore down a rocky mountain, a tyre would go bust. For such earth-moving equipment, each tyre roughly costs ₹60,000. When you consider the rate at which tyres have to be replaced, you realize that this makes up a sizeable portion of the already significant maintenance cost.

Therefore, every tyre that bursts is a regret for my father, another moment of frustration. But over the years, with his experience and with over 250 such trucks and trailers, he has come to believe that this cost is simply a necessary evil, recurring and expensive. The costs are outweighed by the profit he makes by running his business smoothly. Such costs are part and parcel of operations; you simply bear the cost and move on.

For us, such burst tyres have become synonymous with learning how to cope with setbacks. It teaches us to keep persevering despite the odds. Instead of looking at every burst tyre as a roadblock, we need to look at them as speed bumps. Sure, they may slow us down, but they are not insurmountable. Once we accept the constant presence of speed bumps in our lives, we can adapt ourselves to confront any challenge.

My mother once had to organize a fundraiser event for a local charity. She brought together friends to curate an event and have the women in her social club participate to raise funds. All the proceeds from the ticket sales were to be donated to a local children's hospital. The event was a grand success: it raised a respectable amount of funds, created awareness about issues facing maternal and children's health, and brought women together for some fun social and professional networking.

By the end of the evening, my mother realized she had misplaced her cellphone. With all her running around, and with dozens of people moving in and out all night, there was no way to find it. That night, she animatedly recounted the successful event to my father. She was elated she had pulled off such an event on her own. My father congratulated her. As she retired to bed, however, the loss of her phone remained at the back of her mind. Of course, it was nothing compared to her achievements, and one easily misplaced things during large gatherings. She let out a sigh and whispered aloud, '*Mai samjhungi ki ek tyre phat gaya* (I will simply tell myself that a tyre went bust).' It was only then she got some peace of mind. She had let the loss out of her mind.

Our family often uses this quote to remind ourselves that an error is never the end of the world. No matter what happens, life goes on. Given the sheer number of decisions we all have to make daily, the probability of screwing up, failing, losing, misplacing, and miscalculating – you name it – is quite high. But instead of beating ourselves up over our shortcomings – in other words, regretting our actions and their outcomes – it sometimes helps to consider them as the cost of doing business (whether in our lives or our careers) and moving on.

Fixation

धोबी के घुस गये चोर , लुट गये और ही और

Dhobi ke ghus gaye chor, lut gaye aur hi aur
(If the washerman's shop is broken into, it is not his
clothes that are stolen)

A short story about a local laundromat teaches us about letting go and not sweating the small stuff, especially when the situation is not in our hands in the first place.

A thief lived on the outskirts of Hisar. Every once in a while, when he was running low on food and money, he would take a trip into town to steal what he could find. And though everyone knew what he did, the townsfolk could not stop him from pilfering their goods, businesses, and homes. One night, the thief decided to rob the town's laundromat, hoping to sell the clothes to make some quick cash.

Although the meticulous owner had locked up his shop carefully, the laundromat's deadbolts were not enough to deter the thief. Cloaked by the dark of the night, the thief broke the locks and grabbed as many clothes as he could find. When the owner came in the next morning, he was distraught to find his business completely looted, with nothing but a few undergarments and socks left behind. Devastated by the loss, the owner stepped onto the street and began to howl about the thief who had robbed him bare.

As he wailed outside, Ashwani, known to all as the local 'wise guy', happened to pass by. He asked him what the fuss was about. After the owner recounted his story, Ashwani told him, 'But why are you upset? Your clothes haven't been stolen! Those whose clothes were stolen should be upset, not you! Cheer up, the thief didn't take anything you own!

The owner still had his shop, his machines, and his livelihood; indeed, he did not lose anything except perhaps the trust of his customers, which he could regain as everyone would understand that it was the thief who was to blame. The robbery was out of the owner's control, but more importantly, he did not lose anything which belonged to him.

The fable teaches us a powerful lesson about control. We need to worry about and try to change only what we can control. A simpler way to adopt this perspective is by thinking if you owe the bank $100, it is your problem, but if you owe the bank a million, it is the bank's problem. This is not to say we should take responsibility or debt lightly. Rather, this allows us to put things in perspective and regain our confidence in difficult times. Often, you are not in a situation alone; it is not just your loss. Other stakeholders could be consulted, such as family members, employees, suppliers, and clients. Sometimes, looking at the issue from the perspective of other stakeholders can clarify the situation.

We often get caught up in the details and do not see the big picture. We may grow anxious about things that *may* happen or past scenarios that *may* impact us. But most of the time, these are not the things hindering our success. The key is to take a bird's eye view and figure out what we can and cannot control. At that point, it often becomes evident that we may have lost something that was not even ours, to begin with, and thus, we should not pull ourselves down too much.

Naivety

माँ मर गई अँधेरे में बेटा रोशनलाल

Maa mar gayi andhere mein, beta roshan lal
(Mother dies in darkness, while her son is out there
promoting light)

All that glitters is not gold. The above-mentioned
Haryanvi adage says something similar using characteristic
Haryanvi sarcasm: a son bragging to the whole world
how he can bring light anywhere, while his mother lay at
home dying in darkness. So, what he was projecting to the
outside world was far removed from the truth. This saying
also reminds us that we must do our due diligence before
taking a decision or making a choice. Something might
look good superficially, but turn out to be quite different
from what you expected. There have been several instances
when I have found that claims made by marketing agents,
fancy websites, or salespeople were far removed from the
truth. People often exaggerate their success stories since
they think they can get away with anything if they act
confidently, use complex vocabulary, or present bloated
numerical data to support their case.

While every sales pitch is not a sham, do your due
diligence nonetheless. Try not to take any claim at face
value. As a Russian proverb advises, *always* verify. In family

businesses, I find that reference checks can be a quick and smart way to do this when it comes to hiring new talent or adopting a new product. Ask around, make a few calls. The chances that someone else knows the person or has used the product are high, and their feedback may save you a lot of trouble. Any genuine vendor will appreciate this opportunity as well. Do the required background research. Anyone can make up numbers and success stories, so you have to check the viability of a proposal for yourself. Don't be afraid to ask for references, conduct site visits, or run pilots before making a firm plan.

Exasperation

ऊँट यूँही लदते रहेंगे, यूँही अरड़ाते रहेंगे

Unth yuhin ladte rahenge, yunhi radradate rahenge
(The camels will continue to squabble even as they
continue to transport goods)

Persistent whining inevitably falls on deaf ears. Most people complain when they do not want to do something, even if it does not make the task any easier, or any quicker. But folks often complain just for the sake of complaining, thinking it will somehow make things better.

When you are on the receiving end, you may find yourself exasperated and at your wits' end. In the animal world, camels act in quite the same way. They perpetually rumble, a growl that is annoying to human ears. They can be found moaning and groaning all day long – whether they are being loaded with goods or are simply lying down to rest. Long accustomed to the sounds made by their livestock, the traders of Rajasthan and Haryana are unfazed by the camels' groans. Instead, they simply go about their usual business unperturbed. As long as the work gets done, the whimpers, grumbles, and all do not matter at all. Although patience and experience are certainly needed to drown out the whining, traders have one goal that keeps them going: to move their goods. If they can accomplish this by the end of the day, the journey (no matter how frustrating) is of little importance.

The same can be applied to a professional environment. We may find that team members respond unenthusiastically when faced with additional workload. This is quite natural, for people want to maximize their efficiency by expending as little effort as they can. In other words, how can one do the least amount of work and make the most money? Aiming for this could be the recipe for low productivity and output from the team. However, during busy times when employees are asked to step up beyond their normal duties, one may encounter objections, protests, and dissent. It is in your best interest to push ahead, despite the whining, to deliver the results. If the employees will grumble anyway, it does not matter how the work gets done.

Those with children may have experienced a similar situation at home when trying to wrangle their kids into completing their chores, picking up their toys, getting dressed, brushing their teeth, doing their homework, or going to bed. How many times have parents pulled their hair out in frustration at the relentless opposition of their children when it comes to the most menial tasks? Chances are this has happened countless times. At the same time, parents have also discovered that despite the tears, fits, moans, and groans, they can get their children to complete their responsibilities as long as they are ready to bear some huffing and puffing. Indeed, with the promise of perhaps some TV time, a treat, or an outing, clever parents (or perhaps those at their wits' end) can incentivize their children to do their chores. The whining is a nuisance, but it is also inevitable. If you need the task done, better to get it done with the whimpering than not have it done at all.

These diverse examples tell us that if we need something done, we must make it happen. Do not subsidize the work or its quality just because someone is giving you grief for it. If those who you work with do not change how they behave, it is not worth exerting the effort to get them to stop before starting the work. Remind yourself of the do-or-die spirit and just go ahead and do it anyway. While it may require an extra dose of patience on your end, that is a small price to pay to accomplish your goals on time.

Name and Fame

एक काम नाम के लिये और एक काम दाम के लिये

Ek kaam naam ke liye aur ek kaam daam ke liye
(You need two types of jobs, one for fame and
one for money)

Sometimes businesses need to fulfil their bread-and-butter requirements by doing not-so-glamorous jobs while they use the funds generated towards another venture that will bring them fame. Say you have a job you are not particularly in love with. It is nothing to write home about and certainly nothing prestigious, but it pays well and keeps the roof over your head by offering you a steady income and the time to plan your own business. You may not love the job, but if it can be the vehicle through which you achieve your dreams. You may have to swallow your pride and accept the trade-off.

I had a friend in New York named Stephanie, who was a talented Theatre Studies major. She tried out all possible auditions to get acting gigs on Broadway. It was difficult to survive in New York City, pay the rent, and buy outfits and accessories for the auditions. To support her acting career, Stephanie worked as a part-time tour guide. While many may consider it to be a downmarket job, it allowed for Stephanie to hone her street theatre and storytelling skills. Moreover, it paid well, and because she was good at it, she collected generous tips. Stephanie was instinctively jugaadu, able to handle multiple responsibilities at once. Her side gig supported her passion for acting. Acting was for *naam*, while being a tour guide paid the *daam*.

Which business leader does not want to be successful? Indeed, every business leader's dream is to see their ads in the papers, their products in stores, hear people mention their brand, and become a leading name in their field. Being the biggest and the best is an irreplaceable feeling. But often the reality is that without any cash, fame does not last very long. This is why cash, not fame, is king.

For the Haryanvi businessperson, profit is the ultimate reality. The younger generation is often attracted to glamorous jobs, despite not having years of experience and wisdom to know what really matters. They need to be reminded that financial viability is key. There is no shame in pursuing something for money or fame. However, what you pursue for fame should not necessarily be something you expect to make money from, and vice versa. Identify and establish what pursuits will get you the outcome – money or fame – so your expectations can be managed. When we apply this idea to family businesses, we see that it is often the 'underdog' business that brings in the real cash. The next gen must find a way to use existing business set-ups as a springboard for diverse new-age ventures. It can also mean that at times we may need to keep a steady job elsewhere as we slowly try our hand at business.

Embarrassment

भामै ही कोनी।

Bhamme hi koni
(To remain unaffected; to not let things get to
you easily)

Try to not be bogged down by difficult situations. Failure can be debilitating, especially for the new generation entering a business. Failure can cause tremendous anxiety and embarrassment. I have struggled with it both at work and in my personal life far more than I would like to admit. It has taken me years to learn to accept failure and live with it, to come to terms with the effort and time spent even when things do not go according to plan, and to admit that although I could have done things differently, I cannot change the past.

Do not let things get to you and develop a resilient mindset. Once you do so, you will not be weighed down by failures. The more you go with the flow, the easier it will be to surmount various obstacles life puts in your path. Adapt quickly and get back in the game. Reminiscing about spilt milk will only slow you down. Of course, it's incredibly difficult to rise after failing and face the consequent embarrassment and even shame. But this is when your pillars of strength, your family, or your friends, will be of support and help you prepare your armour for the next attempt.

Whenever I would take responsibility for a screw-up, my father would calmly say, 'Beta, *mere toh bhaamme hi koni* – I am not affected by this at all.' Literally, it means to not feel anything, to not care, to remain unaffected. This does not mean my father is disinterested in my failures – far from it. Rather, what he means is that there are far more important things to worry about in life, so if he is not worried, I should not be either.

One of the best things about this idiom is its scalability. We may use it to mitigate the impact of a big screw-up and to have the load of failure taken off our shoulders and feel relieved. I have been touched by my father's ability to forgive and forget. Despite his misgivings or doubts, he has never brought up my failures or discussed them with anyone else, showing his ability to absorb the shock and react with patience, kindness, and empathy.

For the younger generation, waking up to how their failures will be perceived can often be quite daunting. It should fall upon the older generations in a family business to create a culture where making mistakes is considered acceptable (and even encouraged – if done with the right intentions) and where the younger employees can feel comfortable to admit and discuss failures. The reason I saved this adage for the end is because it is my favourite and means that my father always has my back.

Much in life is uncertain: who you will marry, what job you will end up with, and what you will accomplish. What is certain, however, is that risk and failure will always be a part of life. I do not mean to suggest that risk and failure will plague every experience in your life. Rather, my advice is to be prepared to have them appear sporadically through your personal and professional trajectories. Their inevitability may evoke a whole host of emotions such as anxiety, worry, and fear, which is perfectly normal. But you are not doomed to feel these things forever. If you choose to take life into your own hands and implement the tools we have covered in this book, you will find that the challenges brought on by risk and failure are not insurmountable after all.

6

FAMILY BUSINESS IN THE POST-PANDEMIC ERA

'Beta, agle ke kaan hain, toh baat ander jayegi hi.'
'But, papa, what if they don't listen?'
'If you speak, they will listen.'

EVER SINCE I WAS A LITTLE GIRL, MY FATHER HAS encouraged me to speak my mind (how very Haryanvi of him!). He has also taught me the value of asking for what's due to me, to speak up if I want someone to listen. The person I'm talking to may choose to respond or not – it's their prerogative – but unless I clearly communicate what I need or want, I am not helping my chances of getting closer to my goals. A successful Haryanvi businessperson knows that if you don't ask, you don't get. My father taught me to ask so that I could get, and I've become a better businesswoman for it. And I will forever be grateful for this simple yet incredible lesson.

This book has been my way of speaking my mind. It is equally an endeavour to encourage you to speak yours. All of us have valuable insights and ideas that are waiting to fall on the right ears; it requires a little courage (or guts) on our part to share them. And when you finally take that first step, you will find that your stories resonate with many others. All of us have unique lives with unique trajectories, but we still have much in common, particularly in the world of business. The more we see how we are all alike in terms of the challenges and struggles we face, the easier it will be to keep moving forward. The more we learn and share, the more we appreciate the incredible value of our heritage and how it prepares us to survive and excel in our family businesses. Writing this book opened me up to this reality, and I hope that reading it has done the same for you.

We learned a lot through this exploration of crucial family business survival hacks – an exploration meant to enlighten, inspire, enable, and equip you for future success in your own family business. In chapter 1, I introduced you to my business, my family, and me. We talked about the idea of jugaad and delved into some of my experiences at MPIL. We examined (small to medium-sized) family-managed businesses and the negative stereotypes surrounding them, and learned to look beyond them in chapter 2. In chapter 3 we learned that family-managed SMEs can be viable, successful, *and* sustainable by taking advantage of their unique characteristics, including their knack for frugality or their proclivity towards innovation. In chapter 4, we took a deep dive into the ultimate family business survival kit and the go-to tools that make up this practical model. When you're in a pinch, grab the tool you need from this survival kit, and you'll be able to tackle the challenges in front of you.

Though maligned and stereotyped, the values, ideas, and mindsets of Indian family-managed SMEs can help us get out of sticky situations, prepare for worst-case scenarios, and find new paths to success. These simple yet critical tools – inspired by the equally simple yet useful concept of jugaad – are necessary for any SME, and particularly for family businesses whose unique set-up brings unique challenges (and advantages). Finally, we discussed real-world applications of these tools.

In chapter 5, we confronted two of the greatest fears of business owners and employees: risk and failure. Though inevitable parts of running and working for a business (particularly in SMEs, given their startup-like nature), risk and failure instil fears, doubts, anxieties, and worries in all of us. But by analyzing the common emotional responses and scenarios of risk and failure, especially in the context of a family business, we broke down the obstacles into bite-sized pieces and deconstructed them. We can prepare ourselves to confront risk and failure through a thoughtful application of the toolkit. These two aspects cannot be eliminated; rather, the tools mentioned in the book will enable you to react better and recover from them easily. I have repeatedly recalled the adages discussed in chapter 5 to help me deal with both personal and business problems, move on from mistakes, and feel empowered by my decisions. Though they emerge from Haryanvi culture, their application knows no cultural or geographic bounds and thus can be as useful for any business leader who has hit that inevitable rough patch. Any reader is sure to find a nugget of wisdom they could use and apply to their own personal and professional lives.

I chose to write about SMEs and family businesses not just because of the profound effect my family's business has had on me, but also because these are the most widespread and ubiquitous business set-ups around the world. Though corporates dominate news cycles and stock exchanges, small businesses make up the majority of businesses globally. Family businesses in particular are unique in that they can bring together families, relationships, and communities. Their intergenerational nature necessarily leads them to focus on longevity and sustainability. Their typically small size makes them resourceful and innovative. And though at times more informal than corporations in terms of processes, systems, and structures, there is much we can learn from them. I have tried to capture many such learnings in this book and urge you to remember the lessons you may have learned from your own experiences with family businesses.

My MPIL experience has shaped me in different ways. I am more empathetic and open to quick course corrections. I have learned to become more resilient, analytical, and inventive, thanks to the lessons in jugaad I have learned from my father and my efforts to implement this survival toolkit in my life. Though it took me nearly ten years to get around to writing this book, I knew it was critical to put the proverbial pen to paper and describe the lessons I have learned over the past decade.

As I have mentioned in chapter 4, not every situation will call for the implementation of the survival toolkit. But as the expert in your field, industry, or business, you will know the right time to put these tools into use, an instinct that will only improve with time. The toolkit will equip you and your business to face multiple situations and scenarios, including ones you have never imagined. The toolkit – much like the values it espouses – is flexible, adaptable, portable, and pliable. Use it how you see fit and adjust it to your context.

This toolkit is of particular importance now, given the impact of the Covid-19 pandemic on family businesses around the world. Globally, many such businesses have had to close their doors in the face of a devastating economic recession. Though the pandemic is a Goliath of an adversary, the survival toolkit can give family businesses a lifeline in such a time of crisis – whether it is being more cautious when it comes to spending; correcting course when a unit is bleeding money; or perhaps accelerating innovation to produce new products needed during this unprecedented time. The toolkit allows family businesses to confront the massive economic impact of the pandemic.

Though it is tragic when a firm goes under due to a crisis (given the potential job loss and market impact), it is especially so when family businesses close their shutters. SMEs are the backbone of most economies, and despite their small size, they play an outsized role in keeping local, regional, and national economies afloat. Such SMEs also constitute a strong network of personal and professional ties that keep communities engaged, active, employed, productive, and connected in a way giant corporations simply cannot. When we eventually arrive in the aftermath of this unprecedented global pandemic, we will need to rebuild quickly. Who better to lead this effort than family businesses?

Family businesses are frugal, creative, resourceful, innovative, adaptable, malleable, and resilient. Unlike corporations that will need to rebuild from the ground up on a large scale, family businesses have the freedom and flexibility to regroup and rebuild in a more agile way. Moreover, given the fact that family businesses typically do not have a governing board, its leadership has more independence to make critical decisions needed to adjust to changing market realities. Corporations may try to guarantee shareholder value first and foremost during the crisis, but family businesses, by their very nature, focus not only on their bottom line but also on their employees and long-term sustainability. These businesses are used to tough times, risks, and failures, and though this pandemic might be the biggest crisis they have ever faced, they are best equipped to play an important role post pandemic globally, and especially in India.

We've also seen family businesses in India respond innovatively to the pandemic. Some have pivoted assembly lines to produce personal protective equipment, ventilators, and other essential medical products. The Poonawalla family's Serum Institute of India has emerged as the largest vaccine producer in the world. Millions of kirana stores across India have provided families with essential food and goods, as online platforms and big-box stores struggle to keep up with the demand. Thousands of crores of funds were raised to fight the spread of Covid through the efforts of family enterprises by groups such as the Marico Group, the JSW Group, the Vedanta Group and the House of Anita Dongre.[1] These examples illustrate the incredible ability of family businesses to adapt quickly and innovate. Their compassion and family-minded approach also make them retain as many jobs as possible, given how deeply the communities they work with rely on the employment provided by them. And they are often critical parts of supply and value chains. When the pandemic finally begins to recede, family businesses should and will be at the forefront of economic rebuilding. By then, hopefully, all firms regardless of size will have learned to be more resilient, adaptable, lean, and creative – they can all take cues from family businesses. Rebuilding will necessarily have to start small; it is impossible to reignite a national economy at once. Thankfully, family businesses are well placed to carry out this role. Once India begins emerging from the pandemic, we will see small businesses carrying the torch to revitalize their communities. As these communities become stronger, so will the nation.

Family businesses do not always get the attention or support they deserve, despite their contributions to the economy and community. Local, regional, and national policymakers should take note and see how they can enhance the resilience of such businesses going forward, particularly in the event of future global economic shocks. Family businesses and SMEs are the backbones of many local economies and communities. By putting the right regulations and enablers in place, policymakers can ensure the longevity of these businesses. I have jotted down some policy recommendations that I have gathered from my various interactions and interviews during the process of writing this book.

- Out-of-court mediation sessions for family members in conflict or dispute: While mediation is sometimes allowed by the court, or sought by both parties mutually, there is no formal set-up for the same in India which specializes in family business disputes. Such a qualified space would be more equipped to deal with a sibling and/or cousin conflicts, minus the intensity of the court system.
- Mandatory succession plans: Most Indian businesses lack a succession plan, and this is a point of concern when it comes to the maintenance of their legacy and ensuring their continuity. If mandated by the government, these businesses will be compelled to draft one formally which will facilitate a smooth transition of power and control from one generation to another.
- Formal stewardship for the next gens joining a family business: For the next generation to have proper training and a roadmap to enter and eventually lead the family business, guidelines for stewardship should be put in place by the government to ensure that the previous generation has a way to pass down their knowledge and experiences in a structured manner.
- Guidelines and structure for the family office: Most families take care of wealth management and investments on their own and generally outside the formal family office. These families could greatly benefit from a policy

framework prescribing a structure that incentivizes the consolidation of investment efforts and transparency in the business.

- Better financial access and sources of capital for startups and smaller family businesses: This ensures that family businesses have access to modern fundraising channels, at competitive interest rates, allowing them to start businesses as a small team of family members.
- More stable rules and regulations across different government parties: This will allow family businesses to enjoy a stable set of rules and guidelines that are not subjected to changes in the arena of politics. Just as family businesses rely on a long-term mindset, the rules governing them should also be of similar nature so that they remain relevant in the multi-generational context.
- Recognition and respect for family businesses as an industry in their own right: Recognizing their contributions will ensure the continuity of these businesses, which form the very backbone of our economy. Their concerns and specific needs warrant them special consideration on policy decisions.

Corporate enterprises must also take note. The experiential, creative, and prudent approach of family businesses holds important lessons for corporates which may not think twice about some key components including employee development, frugality, and innovation. The future is in supporting local production and less reliance on imports. The spotlight will be back on family businesses as leaders of the 'Vocal for Local' movement.

I hope I have successfully demonstrated why family businesses are important and why we should pay them special attention. If you are a family business owner, I hope you found this book useful and will now be able to identify diverse opportunities to implement the family business survival toolkit wherever and whenever you can. Going by my own experience, I can guarantee that it will change your professional trajectory for the better.

ACKNOWLEDGEMENTS

I am a luck-dominant individual, attracting giants whose shoulders have offered me privilege and opportunity way beyond my reach.

Firstly, I would like to thank my mother Darshana Gupta for always saying yes and for being the best girlfriend ever. And my brother Alok whose noble voice is in my head, urging me to rethink all my assumptions.

I am so thankful to my undergraduate professor Mab Segrest for editing early drafts in detail, to my literary agent Kanishka Gupta for always being on point, and to my commissioning editor Teesta Guha Sarkar for her continuous support towards this book.

Immense thanks to my husband Richard Zielinski for the rock that he is and for allowing me to believe that I can, truly, have it all. I am also thankful to our three kids Henry, Radhika and Savi who have helped out by scattering paper all over the house and offering much-needed distractions.

And finally, this book is an ode to everything I have learned from my father Ashwani Gupta. Thanking him is my lifelong honour.

NOTES

1. Why My Family Business Matters

1. Navi Rajdou, Jaideep Prabhu and Simon Ahuja, 'Jugaad: The Gutsy Art of Improvising an Ingenious Solution,' in *Jugaad Innovation: A Frugal and Flexible Approach to Innovation for the 21st Century* (Random Business, 2012), Kindle.
2. 'India and the Credit Crisis,' *The Economist*, 14 October 2008, http://www.economist.com/node/12411151.
3. Government of India, Rajya Sabha, *Global Economic Crisis and Its Impact on India* (New Delhi: June 2009), 33, https://rajyasabha.nic.in/rsnew/publication_electronic/glob_eco_crisis2009.pdf.
4. Michael E. Porter and Klaus Schwab, *The Global Competitiveness Report 2008–2009* (Geneva: World Economic Forum), 14. http://www3.weforum.org/docs/WEF_GlobalCompetitivenessReport_2008-09.pdf.
5. Shelley Singh, 'How Family-Run Businesses Are Evolving Amid Innovation and the Startup Invasion,' *Economic Times*, 12 December 2017, https://economictimes.indiatimes.com/small-biz/startups/features/how-family-run-businesses-

are-evolving-amid-innovation-and-the-startup-invasion/
articleshow/62029085.cms?from=mdr.

6. 'India's 10 Oldest Family-owned Businesses.' siliconindia,
   10 February 2014, https://www.siliconindia.com/news/
   business/Indias-10-Oldest-Family-Owned-Businesses-nid-
   161024-cid-3.html.

7. *PwC's Family Business Survey 2012-2013: Family Firm the
   India Perspective*, https://www.pwc.in/assets/pdfs/family-
   business-survey/family-business-survey-2013.pdf.

8. Ruchir Sharma, 'Breakout or Washout,' in *Reimagining India:
   Unlocking the Potential of Asia's Next Superpower*, (New York:
   Simon & Schuster, 2013), Kindle.

9. Jim Lee, 'Family Firm Performance: Further Evidence,'
   Family Business Review 19, no. 2 (2006): pp. 103-114, https://
   doi.org/10.1111/j.1741-6248.2006.00060.x.

2. Why All Family Businesses Matter

1. Peter Cappelli et al., 'Indian Business Rising: The
   Contemporary Indian Way of Conducting Business,'
   in *The India Way How India's Top Business Leaders Are
   Revolutionizing Management*, (Boston: Harvard Business
   Review Press, 2014), Kindle.

2. Shelley Singh. 'Next Gen Must Imbibe Founders Mentality
   to Thrive: Nikhil Ojha, Bain & Company.' *Economic Times*,
   13 December 2017, https://economictimes.indiatimes.
   com/opinion/interviews/next-gen-must-imbibe-
   founders-mentality-to-thrive-nikhil-ojha-bain-company/
   articleshow/62050384.cms?from=mdr.

3. Ibid.

4. Pramodita Sharma and Allan Cohen, 'Secrets of Successful Entrepreneurial Leaders,' in *Entrepreneurs in Every Generation How Successful Family Businesses Develop Their Next Leaders* (Oakland: Berrett-Koehler Publishers, 2016), Kindle.

5. Cappelli, 'Indian Business Rising: The Contemporary Way of Conducting Business,' in *The India Way*.

6. Barry Jaruzelski, John Loehr, and Richard Holman, 'The Global Innovation 1000: Why Culture Is Key,' strategy+business, 25 October 2011, https://www.strategy-business.com/article/11404?gko=62080.

7. 'World Bank SME Finance,' World Bank, https://www.worldbank.org/en/topic/smefinance.

8. Joe C. Mathew, 'Family Businesses Contribute over 70% to India's GDP, Says Farhad Forbes of Family Business Network,' *Business Today*, 9 September 2019, https://www.businesstoday.in/opinion/interviews/family-businesses-contribute-over-70-to-india-gdp-says-farhad-forbes-of-family-business-network/story/378135.html.

9. *PwC's Family Business Survey 2012-2013*.

10. *Credit Suisse Research Institute: The CS Family 1000 Report (2018)*, September 2018, 5.

11. *PwC India Family Business Survey 2019*, 4, https://www.pwc.in/assets/pdfs/research-insights/fbs/2019/pwc-india-family-business-survey-2019.pdf.

12. 'Serum Institute to Begin Trials of Oxford's Covid-19 Vaccine by August-End,' *Business Standard*, 21 July 2020), https://www.business-standard.com/article/current-affairs/serum-institute-to-begin-oxford-s-covid-19-vaccine-trials-by-august-end-120072102004_1.html.

13. Anurima. 'Keeping the Hopes High amidst COVID-19:

Yash Dongre,' Apparel Resources, 8 August 2020. https://
apparelresources.com/fashion-news/features/keeping-
hopes-high-amidst-covid-19-yash-dongre/.

14. Shelley Singh, 'How Family-Run Businesses Are Evolving.'

15. *PwC India Family Business Survey 2019*, 22.

16. A. Lyman, et al, 'Women in Family Business: An Untapped
    Resource,' quoted in Francesca Maria Cesaroni and Annalisa
    Sentuti, 'Women and Family Businesses. When Women Are
    Left Only Minor Roles,' The History of the Family vol 19, no.
    3 (March 2014): 358–379, https://doi.org/10.1080/108160
    2x.2014.929019.

17. Cathleen (Folker) Leitch, 'Women in Family Firms:
    Characteristics, Roles, and Contributions,' Small Business
    Institute® Research Review, proceedings of the Small
    Business Institute® Annual Conference (2008) 35, 157-
    168, Women in Family Business E-Book (Insights) https://
    dorisscheibenbogen.com/wp-content/uploads/2017/10/
    Insights_Women_in_Family_Business_E_book.pdf.

18. Ibid.

19. 'Women in Leadership: The Family Business Advantage
    Special Report Based on a Global Survey of the World's
    Largest Family Businesses (2014),' Family Business Center of
    Excellence, 2015, 3, https://familybusiness.ey-vx.com/pdfs/
    ey-women-in-leadership-the-family-business-advantage.
    pdf.

20. Yashodhara Basuthakur and Nupur Pavan Bang. 'Redefining
    the Role of Women in Indian Family Businesses,' ISBInsight,
    27 August 2019, https://isbinsight.isb.edu/redefining-the-
    role-of-women-in-indian-family-businesses/.

21. Ibid.

3. Reclaiming Family Businesses

1. *Family Businesses in India: Transforming Organizations to Unlock Unrealized Potential*, Alvarez & Marsal, 2018.
2. Sumant Batra, 'The Changing Face of Family Business in India,' Campden FB, 1 February 2002, http://www.campdenfb.com/article/changing-face-family-business-india
3. *Credit Suisse Report 2018*, 6.
4. Capelli, 'Indian Business Rising' in *The India Way*.
5. Anu Raghunathan, 'Lavanya Nalli Wants Family Silks Business to Be No.1 Global Sari Destination,' *Forbes*, 10 April 2016, https://www.forbes.com/sites/anuraghunathan/2016/04/06/lavanya-nalli-wants-to-make-her-silks-business-the-no-1-global-sari-destination/#67258ae253fe.
6. John A. Davis, 'Professionalizing the Family Business: It's Not What You Think It Is,' CFEG Main, 20 August 2020, https://cfeg.com/insights_research/professionalizing-the-family-business-its-not-what-you-think-it-is/.
7. Rekha Balakrishnan, 'How a Woman from a Conservative Family Went on to Achieve Rs 1,000 Cr Revenue for McDonald's in India,' YourStory.com, 11 March 2020, https://yourstory.com/herstory/2020/03/woman-entrepreneur-mcdonalds-india.

4. The Ultimate Family Business Survival Kit

1. Suparna Dutt, 'Innovation: Can India Escape the Jugaad Trap?,' *Gulf News*, 29 October 2018, http://gulfnews.com/gn-focus/country-guides/reports/india/innovation-can-india-escape-the-jugaad-trap-1.1877592.

2. Shelley Singh, 'How Family-Run Businesses Are Evolving.'

3. Sheryl Sandberg and Nell Scovell, 'The Myth of Doing It All,' in *Lean in: Women, Work, and the Will to Lead* (New York: Alfred A. Knopf, 2019), Kindle.

4. Pramodita Sharma and Allan Cohen, 'Secrets of Successful Entrepreneurial Leaders,' in *Entrepreneurs in Every Generation*.

6. Saurabh Deshpande, 'How Akshay Modi Turned around the Family Business with Modi Naturals,' YourStory.com, 20 January 2014, https://yourstory.com/2014/01/modi-naturals?utm_pageloadtype=scroll.

6. Tina Fey, *Bossypants* (New York: Little, Brown, 2013), 72.

7. Timothy F. Slaper and Tanya J. Hall, 'The Triple Bottom Line: What Is It and How Does It Work?,' Indian Business Review, https://www.ibrc.indiana.edu/ibr/2011/spring/article2.html.

8. Samit Aich, 'Triple Bottom Line: A Bridge between Corporate Capitalism and Deliberate Socialism?,' Medium, 18 March 2019, https://medium.com/s3idf/triple-bottom-line-a-bridge-between-corporate-capitalism-and-deliberate-socialism-90bcac79e29c.

9. Anil Dharker, *The Man Who Talked to Machines: The Story of Om Prakash Jindal* (Mumbai: Eminence Designs Pvt. Ltd, 2005), 120.

10. Rashmi Menon, 'In 1984, I Was Newly Married, Had No Money and Hated Borrowing from My Dad: Sajjan Jindal,' *Economic Times*, 13 December 2017, https://economictimes.indiatimes.com/magazines/panache/in-1984-i-was-newly-married-had-no-money-and-hated-borrowing-from-my-dad-sajjan-jindal/articleshow/62048140.cms?from=mdr.

11. Biswarup Gooptu, 'Lightbox Invests $8 Million in Apparel Firm Bombay Shirt Company,' *Economic Times*, 12 December 2019, https://economictimes.indiatimes.com/internet/lightbox-invests-8-million-in-apparel-firm-bombay-shirt-company/articleshow/72498863.cms.

12. 'Where Innovation Meets Business,' *Economic Times*, 19 September 2018, https://economictimes.indiatimes.com/familybusinessforum/bangalore-articles-2018/where-innovation-meets-business/articleshow/65868878.cms?utm_source=contentofinterest&utm_medium=text&utm_campaign=cppst.

13. Tom Rath, 'Strengthsfinder: The Next Generation,' in *StrengthsFinder2.0* (Gallup Press, 2007), Kindle.

14. Tina Fey, *Bossypants*, 84.

15. Reid Hoffman and Ben Casnocha, *The Start-up of You: Adapt to the Future, Invest in Yourself, and Transform Your Career* (Cornerstone Digital, 2012), 49, Kindle.

16. Rohan Abraham, 'Harsh Mariwala Talks Product Failure, Importance of Going to Marketplace; Shares Success Story behind Saffola Oats,' *Economic Times*, 1 March 2020, https://economictimes.indiatimes.com/magazines/panache/harsh-mariwala-talks-product-failure-importance-of-going-to-marketplace-shares-success-story-behind-saffola-oats/articleshow/74414681.cms?from=mdr.

17. John P. Kotter, Preface, in *A Sense of Urgency* (Harvard Business Review Press, 2008), Kindle.

18. Ibid.

19. Fey, Tina, *Bossypants*, 123.

5. Surviving Risk and Failure

1. Binjal Shah, 'Anu Aga, India's Eighth Richest Woman, Says She Is No Different from You,' YourStory.com, 23 March 2016,. https://yourstory.com/2016/03/anu-aga.

2. John A. Davis, Maria Sinanis, and Courtney Collette, 'Developing the Next Generation as Managers,' in *Next Generation Success: Reflections on a Decade of Dialogue between Senior and Junior Generations at Harvard Business School* (Cambridge Family Enterprise Press, 2014), Kindle.

3. Anurima, 'Keeping the Hopes High.'

4. Ibid.

6. Family Business in the Post-Pandemic Era

1. Priya Jaiswal, 'Mukesh Ambani to Ratan Tata: Business Tycoons Who Lead Donations in Battle against Coronavirus,' IndiaTV News, 1 April 2020, https://www.indiatvnews.com/business/news-coronavirus-donation-list-mukesh-ambani-ratan-tata-business-tycoons-contribution-pm-cares-fund-covid-19-602567.

ABOUT THE AUTHOR

Photo credit: Louise van Aarde

Priyanka Gupta Zielinski is a business leader and author. Through her writings, she addresses the biggest pressure points facing the next generation of India: career, love, and marriage. By exploring the role of Indian traditions and repositioning them with a beneficial, modern twist, Priyanka seeks to empower India's next generation in their pursuit of new opportunities and fulfilment in their lives and careers.

As the executive director of MPIL Steel Structures Ltd, Priyanka has led her family business to exponential growth and diversification. She has previously worked with financial institutions such as Women's World Banking and the Fund for the City of New York. In 2012, she was named Woman Entrepreneur of the Year by ET Now.

She holds a bachelor's degree in Economics and Gender and Women's Studies from Connecticut College, a Visiting Fellowship in Development Economics with the University of Oxford, and a master's degree in International Public Finance from New York University.

Priyanka lives in Dubai with her husband and three children.